Getting Started with Python and Raspberry Pi

Learn to design and implement reliable Python applications on Raspberry Pi, using a range of external libraries, the Raspberry Pi's GPIO port, and the camera module

Dan Nixon

[PACKT] open source*

PUBLISHING   community experience distilled

BIRMINGHAM - MUMBAI

Getting Started with Python and Raspberry Pi

First published: September 2015

Production reference: 1210915

Published by Packt Publishing Ltd.
Livery Place
35 Livery Street
Birmingham B3 2PB, UK.

ISBN 978-1-78355-159-0

www.packtpub.com

Credits

Author
Dan Nixon

Reviewers
Ankit Aggarwal
Neil Broers
Yash Gajera
Bhavyanshu Parasher
David Whale

Commissioning Editor
Dipika Gaonkar

Acquisition Editor
Indrajit Das

Content Development Editor
Zeeyan Pinheiro

Technical Editor
Namrata Patil

Copy Editor
Alpha Singh

Project Coordinator
Suzanne Coutinho

Proofreader
Safis Editing

Indexer
Tejal Soni

Graphics
Jason Monteiro

Production Coordinator
Manu Joseph

Cover Work
Manu Joseph

About the Author

Dan Nixon is a software and electronics engineer living in the north of England. He has past experience of creating software for data analysis, process control, and business intelligence applications. In most of these projects, Python was one of the main languages used.

Dan previously authored another book on the uses of the Raspberry Pi, called *Raspberry Pi Blueprints*, and has worked on many personal projects that use both Python and the Raspberry Pi.

I would like to thank my mother and father for their support in writing this book and Greg Fenton for his help in testing some of the examples included.

About the Reviewers

Ankit Aggarwal has been fascinated with science and technology since childhood. He likes to experiment and learn new things. He is a software engineer and researcher by profession and loves computer science. He wants to solve problems using technology. His interests include science, technology, academic research, music, photography, entrepreneurship, DIY, movies, anime, and much more.

He has worked in the fields of networking, distributed systems, pervasive/mobile computing, data science, AI, and computer vision; the list goes on. Ankit has authored IEEE Xplore research papers and is an active contributor to and author of several open source projects. He is socially active, blogs occasionally, and maintains his website at `http://ankitaggarwal.me`.

In his free time, he reads, takes part in competitive programming, captures photos of nature with a lens, and watches TV shows, movies, and anime. When he is not doing these things, he can be found jogging at the nearest ground.

Neil Broers is a Python developer by day and a hardware hacker by night, building his "Smart Home," one Raspberry Pi at a time. He is an avid technical blogger on `www.foo.co.za`, where he documents his adventures with home automation. In 2014, he presented a talk on the Raspberry Pi and the Internet of Things at the PyConZA conference in South Africa.

Yash Gajera is an embedded software engineer at Insignex in Anand, India. He studied electronics and communication engineering and graduated in 2014 from the A. D. Patel Institute of Technology, Anand. At Insignex, he has worked on fully automated irrigation control systems. He did his final year project on the Internet of Things. It was selected as the best project from the EC department at Gujarat Technological University in 2014. Yash wrote a Python library for the Zigbee protocol to work with the Raspberry Pi. He also has a lot of experience in embedded system development and web technologies.

Bhavyanshu Parasher holds a BTech degree in computer science engineering. He is currently working toward getting a master's degree in computer science. He has been developing web applications since 2011. He also has experience in developing apps for Android and Linux. He has authored and contributed to various open source projects. Apart from computer science, he is also interested in electronics. He has developed various projects using the Raspberry Pi, including service bots, weather monitoring systems, and data analysis automation tools. When he is not writing code, he spends time writing tutorials on his blog at `https://bhavyanshu.me`.

David Whale is a software developer living in Essex, UK. He started coding as a schoolboy aged 11, inspired by the school science technician to build his own computer from a kit, and quickly progressed to writing machine code programs because they were "small and fast." These early experiments led to some of his code being used in a saleable educational word game when he was only 13.

David has been developing software professionally ever since, mainly writing small and fast code that goes into electronic products, including automated machinery, electric cars, mobile phones, energy meters, and wireless doorbells.

These days, he runs his own software consultancy called Thinking Binaries. He spends much of his time helping design the next wave of the Internet, called the Internet of Things. This means connecting electronic devices to the Internet. The rest of the time, he volunteers for The Institution of Engineering and Technology, running training courses for teachers, designing and running workshops and clubs for school children, and generally being busy with his Raspberry Pi.

David was the technical editor of the book *Adventures in Raspberry Pi*. He is a coauthor of the book *Adventures in Minecraft* and is the technical editor of the official Raspberry Pi magazine, the *MagPi*.

> I was really pleased to be asked to review this new book. Dan Nixon has done an excellent job of getting you started with Python and your Raspberry Pi, and he presents the material in an easy-to-follow format. There are lots of fun ideas and building blocks here, which I hope many readers will extend into bigger and more ambitious projects of their own.

www.PacktPub.com

Support files, eBooks, discount offers, and more

For support files and downloads related to your book, please visit www.PacktPub.com.

Did you know that Packt offers eBook versions of every book published, with PDF and ePub files available? You can upgrade to the eBook version at www.PacktPub.com and as a print book customer, you are entitled to a discount on the eBook copy. Get in touch with us at service@packtpub.com for more details.

At www.PacktPub.com, you can also read a collection of free technical articles, sign up for a range of free newsletters and receive exclusive discounts and offers on Packt books and eBooks.

https://www2.packtpub.com/books/subscription/packtlib

Do you need instant solutions to your IT questions? PacktLib is Packt's online digital book library. Here, you can search, access, and read Packt's entire library of books.

Why subscribe?

- Fully searchable across every book published by Packt
- Copy and paste, print, and bookmark content
- On demand and accessible via a web browser

Free access for Packt account holders

If you have an account with Packt at www.PacktPub.com, you can use this to access PacktLib today and view 9 entirely free books. Simply use your login credentials for immediate access.

Table of Contents

Preface

The Raspberry Pi is one of the smallest and most affordable single board computers that has taken over the world of hobby electronics and programming, and the Python programming language makes this the perfect platform to start coding with.

Getting Started with Python and Raspberry Pi will guide you through the process of designing, implementing, and debugging your own Python applications to run on the Raspberry Pi and will help you interact with some of its unique hardware.

What this book covers

Chapter 1, Your First Steps with Python on the Pi, introduces the Python development tools as you install and set them up on the Raspberry Pi after installing the Raspbian operating system.

Chapter 2, Understanding Control Flow and Data Types, introduces you to the control flow and conditional execution operations. Also, the basic data types and the operations that can be performed on them will be covered in this chapter.

Chapter 3, Working with Data Structures and I/O, gives you an overview of the standard Python data structures (for example, list, dict, and tuple) and how they can be used within an application. Also, this chapter will provide an introduction to reading and writing files on the Raspberry Pi's filesystem, including reading from the sysfs to get data such as the current temperature of the processor.

Chapter 4, Understanding Object-oriented Programming and Threading, introduces the concept of object-oriented programming and compares it to the functional programming that has been done up to this point in this book.

Chapter 5, Packaging Code with setuptools, introduces you to the setup tools in the Python package, which are used to package Python applications and libraries for easier installation. This will also include an introduction to the pip utility and PyPi package repository.

Chapter 6, Accessing the GPIO Pins, gives you an overview of the Python library for accessing the GPIO pins on the Raspberry Pi and a brief introduction to some basic electronics needed for the tutorials in the chapter.

Chapter 7, Using the Camera Module, covers using the picamera Python library to interact with the camera module, the options that can be configured using the library, and writing a simple application to record a section of video in several different modes.

Chapter 8, Extracting Data from the Internet, covers the use of several libraries (including requests and urllib2) to connect to webservers and request data, and will include obtaining weather forecasts from an online API. Also, you will be introduced to several third-party libraries that access data from specific sources.

Chapter 9, Creating Command-line Interfaces, covers interaction with applications via the command line using the argparse Python module.

Chapter 10, Debugging Applications with PDB and Log Files, introduces you to the PDB (Python debugger) tool, discusses how it can be used to diagnose and fix issues in Python programs, and covers how the logging Python module can be used to capture information from an application to be used later for debugging. This includes a tutorial in which code with several issues placed into it will be debugged and corrected.

Chapter 11, Designing Your GUI with Qt, provides an introduction to GUI design with Qt using Qt Designer and the Python Qt package.

What you need for this book

You will need:

- A Raspberry Pi
- An SD card (4 GB or higher)

Who this book is for

This book is designed for those who are unfamiliar with the art of Python development and want to get to know their way around the language and the many additional libraries that allow you to get a full application up and running in no time.

Conventions

In this book, you will find a number of styles of text that distinguish between different kinds of information. Here are some examples of these styles, and an explanation of their meaning.

Code words in text, database table names, folder names, filenames, file extensions, pathnames, dummy URLs, user input, and Twitter handles are shown as follows: "We can include other contexts through the use of the include directive."

A block of code is set as follows:

```
flan = "495"
flan
type(flan)
flan_i = int(flan)
flan_i
type(flan_i)
```

Any command-line input or output is written as follows:

```
sudo python setup.py install
```

New terms and **important words** are shown in bold. Words that you see on the screen, in menus or dialog boxes for example, appear in the text like this: "Next we will disable the **LineEdit** widget that will be used for displaying the result of a unit conversion, this is done by selecting the widget and removing the tick in the **enabled** property in the **Property Editor** as shown in the following screenshot."

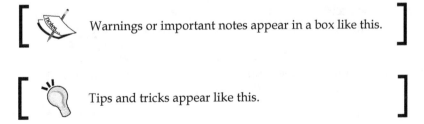

Warnings or important notes appear in a box like this.

Tips and tricks appear like this.

Reader feedback

Feedback from our readers is always welcome. Let us know what you think about this book—what you liked or may have disliked. Reader feedback is important for us to develop titles that you really get the most out of.

To send us general feedback, simply send an e-mail to feedback@packtpub.com, and mention the book title via the subject of your message.

If there is a topic that you have expertise in and you are interested in either writing or contributing to a book, see our author guide on www.packtpub.com/authors.

Customer support

Now that you are the proud owner of a Packt book, we have a number of things to help you to get the most from your purchase.

Downloading the example code

You can download the example code files for all Packt books you have purchased from your account at http://www.packtpub.com. If you purchased this book elsewhere, you can visit http://www.packtpub.com/support and register to have the files e-mailed directly to you.

Errata

Although we have taken every care to ensure the accuracy of our content, mistakes do happen. If you find a mistake in one of our books—maybe a mistake in the text or the code—we would be grateful if you could report this to us. By doing so, you can save other readers from frustration and help us improve subsequent versions of this book. If you find any errata, please report them by visiting http://www.packtpub.com/submit-errata, selecting your book, clicking on the **Errata Submission Form** link, and entering the details of your errata. Once your errata are verified, your submission will be accepted and the errata will be uploaded to our website or added to any list of existing errata under the Errata section of that title.

To view the previously submitted errata, go to https://www.packtpub.com/books/content/support and enter the name of the book in the search field. The required information will appear under the **Errata** section.

Piracy

Piracy of copyright material on the Internet is an ongoing problem across all media. At Packt, we take the protection of our copyright and licenses very seriously. If you come across any illegal copies of our works, in any form, on the Internet, please provide us with the location address or website name immediately so that we can pursue a remedy.

Please contact us at copyright@packtpub.com with a link to the suspected pirated material.

We appreciate your help in protecting our authors, and our ability to bring you valuable content.

Questions

You can contact us at questions@packtpub.com if you are having a problem with any aspect of the book, and we will do our best to address it.

1
Your First Steps with Python on the Pi

In this chapter, we will look at setting up the Raspbian operating system on the Raspberry Pi and have a quick look at the Python development tools that come pre-installed on it, along with looking at some basic ways in which we can execute the Python code.

The only things that are required here are:

- A Raspberry Pi
- A USB power source capable of delivering at least 1A
- USB keyboard
- USB mouse
- TV with HDMI port
- An SD card (or microSD card for the model B+ and Pi 2) of at least 4GB capacity
- An SD card reader
- A USB hub (if you wish to connect more USB devices that there are ports on the Raspberry Pi)
- Optionally, a WiFi adapter if you want to connect the Pi to your network wirelessly (the list of supported USB WiFi adapters is available at elinux.org/RPi_USB_Wi-Fi_Adapters)

Installing and setting up Raspbian

The first thing we need to do is head to the Raspberry Pi downloads page at
`https://www.raspberrypi.org/downloads/` and download the latest version of
Raspbian. This is a version of the Debian Linux distribution, specifically designed
for the Raspberry Pi.

1. On the downloads page select the **Download ZIP** option under **RASPBIAN**.

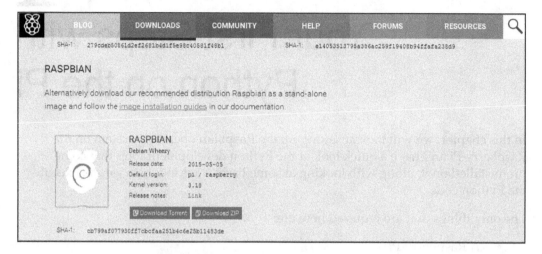

2. Once the file has downloaded, extract the Zip archive using the default
   tool on your **OS**. You should now have a single file ending with the file
   extension `.img`.

Writing to the SD card

The next step is to write the just downloaded operating system image to the SD
card so that it can be used with the Pi. The way this is done varies depending on
the operating system you use on your main PC.

Windows

On Windows, we will use a tool called **Win32 Disk Imager** to write the OS
image to the SD card. This tool can be downloaded from the **SourceForge** page
at `sourceforge.net/projects/win32diskimager`.

1. Once downloaded and installed, insert your SD card and open Win32 Disk
   Imager. You should see a window similar to the following screenshot:

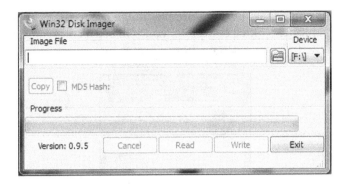

The important thing to check is that a drive letter appears in the **Device** drop down list. If this does not happen then Win32 Disk Imager has failed to recognize your SD card. In such a case, try it in a different SD card reader. If it still does not work then it could indicate that the card has failed.

2. Next, browse to select the `.img` file you had previously extracted from the downloaded Zip archive and click the **Write** button as shown in the following screenshot, after first making sure that the correct device is selected in the **Device** drop down list:

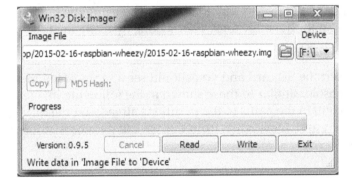

3. You will then see a confirmation dialog similar to the one shown in the next screenshot, asking you to confirm that the image and device are correct. Assuming they are, click on **Yes**.

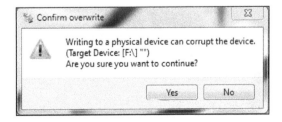

4. Win32 Disk Imager will now write the image file to the SD card. This can take a few minutes. Once complete, you will see a confirmation dialog box as seen in the following screenshot:

You now have Raspbian loaded on the SD card and can now move on to the Boot Pi for the first time. This will be covered in the following sections.

Linux and Mac

On Linux and Mac, the dd command line utility can be used to write the operating system image to the SD card.

1. First, we need to determine the path to the storage device you want to write to. On Linux, the easiest way to do this is by using the udev management tool to monitor the udev logs. This is done by using the following command:

   ```
   udevadm monitor --udev
   ```

2. Now insert the SD card and you should see a series of log messages printed to the console, similar to those shown in the following image. The last few should contain the paths to the partitions already on the drive (in my case, /dev/sdb1 and /dev/sdb2; from this we can deduce that the path to the SD card is /dev/sdb).

```
udevadm  /home/dan
dan@dannixon-envy-ubuntu -> udevadm monitor --udev
monitor will print the received events for:
UDEV - the event which udev sends out after rule processing

UDEV  [774.147490] add       /devices/pci0000:00/0000:00:14.0/usb2/2-2 (usb)
UDEV  [774.162225] add       /module/usb_storage (module)
UDEV  [774.162915] add       /devices/pci0000:00/0000:00:14.0/usb2/2-2/2-2:1.0 (usb)
UDEV  [774.162929] add       /bus/usb/drivers/usb-storage (drivers)
UDEV  [774.162943] add       /devices/pci0000:00/0000:00:14.0/usb2/2-2/2-2:1.0/host6 (scsi)
UDEV  [774.163270] add       /devices/pci0000:00/0000:00:14.0/usb2/2-2/2-2:1.0/host6/scsi_host/host6 (sc
si_host)
UDEV  [775.161862] add       /devices/pci0000:00/0000:00:14.0/usb2/2-2/2-2:1.0/host6/target6:0:0 (scsi)
UDEV  [775.162243] add       /devices/pci0000:00/0000:00:14.0/usb2/2-2/2-2:1.0/host6/target6:0:0/6:0:0:0
(scsi)
UDEV  [775.162665] add       /devices/pci0000:00/0000:00:14.0/usb2/2-2/2-2:1.0/host6/target6:0:0/6:0:0:0
/scsi_disk/6:0:0:0 (scsi_disk)
UDEV  [775.163010] add       /devices/pci0000:00/0000:00:14.0/usb2/2-2/2-2:1.0/host6/target6:0:0/6:0:0:0
/scsi_device/6:0:0:0 (scsi_device)
UDEV  [775.163238] add       /devices/pci0000:00/0000:00:14.0/usb2/2-2/2-2:1.0/host6/target6:0:0/6:0:0:0
/scsi_generic/sg1 (scsi_generic)
UDEV  [775.163790] add       /devices/pci0000:00/0000:00:14.0/usb2/2-2/2-2:1.0/host6/target6:0:0/6:0:0:0
/bsg/6:0:0:0 (bsg)
UDEV  [775.327209] add       /devices/virtual/bdi/8:16 (bdi)
UDEV  [775.424669] add       /devices/pci0000:00/0000:00:14.0/usb2/2-2/2-2:1.0/host6/target6:0:0/6:0:0:0
/block/sdb (block)
UDEV  [775.468264] add       /devices/pci0000:00/0000:00:14.0/usb2/2-2/2-2:1.0/host6/target6:0:0/6:0:0:0
/block/sdb/sdb1 (block)
UDEV  [775.523652] add       /devices/pci0000:00/0000:00:14.0/usb2/2-2/2-2:1.0/host6/target6:0:0/6:0:0:0
/block/sdb/sdb2 (block)
```

3. Next, we need to ensure that none of the existing partitions are mounted before we try to write to the SD card. This can be done by running the following command for every partition discovered using `udevadm`:

`umount PATH`

Here PATH is the path to the partition. This should give an output similar to the following image if the partition was not mounted; otherwise the command will exit without printing any output:

```
fish  /home/dan
dan@dannixon-envy-ubuntu -> umount /dev/sdb1
umount: /dev/sdb1 is not mounted (according to mtab)
dan@dannixon-envy-ubuntu -> umount /dev/sdb2
umount: /dev/sdb2 is not mounted (according to mtab)
dan@dannixon-envy-ubuntu ->
```

4. At this point, the SD card is ready to be written to. For this we will use the following command:

    ```
    sudo dd if=[path to .img] of=[path to SD]
    ```

    Here [path to .img] is the path to the .img file extracted from the Zip archive downloaded earlier and [path to SD] is the path to the SD card we just discovered.

    This process will take some time (up to 20 minutes) and is complete when the command exits and you see the next shell prompt as shown in the following screenshot. If the writing fails then an error message will be printed to the terminal.

```
dan@dannixon-envy-ubuntu ~> sudo dd if=2015-02-16-raspbian-wheezy.img of=/dev/sdb
[sudo] password for dan:
6400000+0 records in
6400000+0 records out
3276800000 bytes (3.3 GB) copied, 1046.11 s, 3.1 MB/s
dan@dannixon-envy-ubuntu ~> 
```

Booting the Pi for the first time

Now that you have an SD card with Raspbian installed on it, you are ready to boot the Pi for the first time and perform the first time configuration steps required to get the Pi up and running.

Note that to fully setup the Pi, you will need to have a way to connect it to the internet in order to install and update the software packages. This can either be wired (using an Ethernet cable) or wireless (using a USB WiFi adapter).

1. Firstly, connect the mouse, keyboard, monitor, and either the WiFi adapter or the Ethernet cable to the Pi. Insert the SD card and connect a USB power source. You should see the red PWR **LED (Light Emitting Diode)** light up and shortly after that, the green ACT LED would start to blink.

    Note that the USB power source should be able to supply at least 1.5A to ensure reliable operation of the Pi. Usually, the USB chargers supplied with the tablets are a good choice of power supply.

2. Once the Pi has booted, you will see the configuration utility as shown in the following screenshot. The first thing we need to do here is to expand the root partition on the SD card to fill the entire SD card. This ensures that we have the maximum space available once we start using the Pi. This is done by selecting the **Expand Filesystem** option at the top of the list and pressing *Enter*.

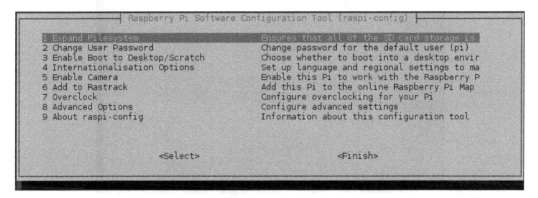

3. Once the filesystem has been modified, you will see a message similar to the one shown next. Press *Enter* to return to the main menu.

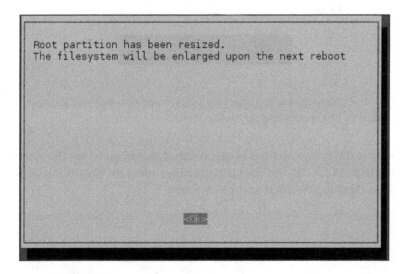

4. Next, we will change the password for the default Pi user. This is done by selecting the second option on the main menu, **Change User Password**, and pressing *Enter*.

5. You will now see a message box similar to the one shown next, with instructions on entering a new password. Press *Enter* to continue.

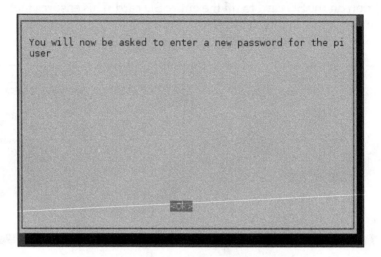

6. You will now be required to enter a new password. Press *Enter* when finished. Once you have done this, you will be asked to enter the password again to confirm.

 Note that when entering a password you will not see any characters appear on the screen.

7. Now that the password has been changed, we need to set the default boot action to start LXDE, the desktop manager used on Raspbian. Select **Enable Boot to Desktop/Scratch** and press *Enter*.

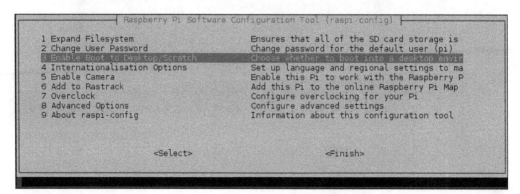

8. Now select the second Desktop option and press *Enter*.

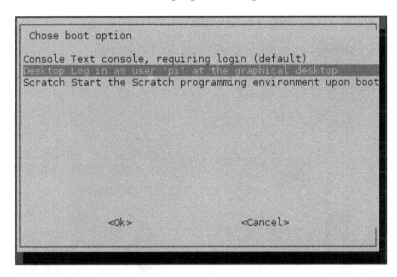

```
Chose boot option

Console Text console, requiring login (default)
Desktop Log in as user 'pi' at the graphical desktop
Scratch Start the Scratch programming environment upon boot




                    <Ok>                        <Cancel>
```

9. You may also wish to change the default locale using the **Internationalisation Options** menu option. By default, the Pi is configured for the UK.

10. Once you are ready to reboot the Pi to apply all of the new settings. This is done by selecting the **Finish** option and pressing *Enter*.

11. You will be asked for a confirmation that you want to reboot. Select **Yes** and press *Enter*.

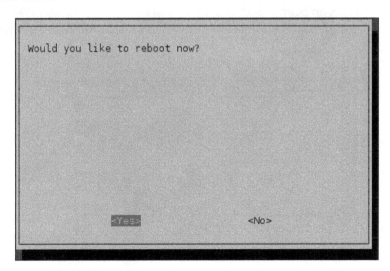

```
Would you like to reboot now?




                  <Yes>                          <No>
```

12. If you are using Ethernet to connect to your network then you can skip this step. Otherwise, we will now setup the WiFi adapter and connect to a wireless network.

   1. Open `wpa_gui` by choosing the **WiFi Configuration** utility in the **Preferences** submenu from the main menu in Raspbian.

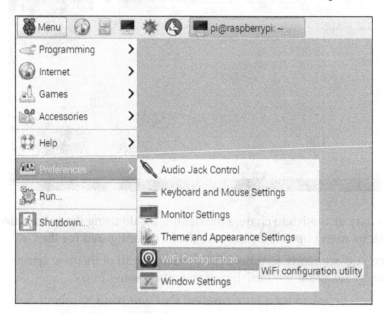

   2. Click on **Scan** to search for wireless networks in range. When complete, you should see a list similar to the one in the following screenshot:

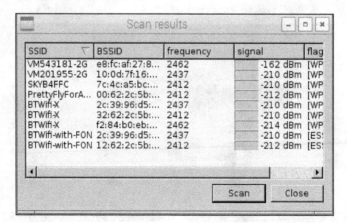

3. When the scan completes, double click on the WiFi network you wish to connect to and you will be shown a window similar to the one in the following image, with some of the details of the network filled in:

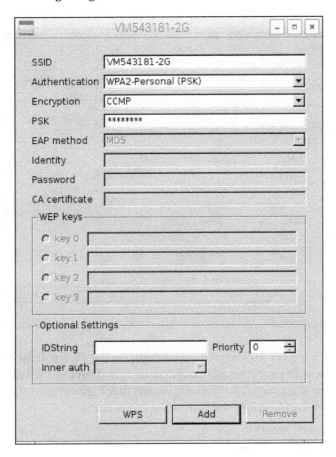

4. Here all that is usually needed to be done is to enter the WiFi password in the **PSK** field and click on **Add**.

5. When done, the network should be selected in the **Network** drop down box automatically. Now click on **Connect** to connect to the network. Assuming all went well, you should see the **Status** of the connection show **Connected**, as shown in this next screenshot:

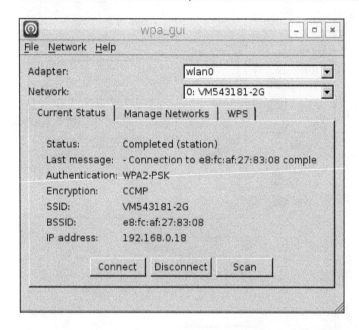

13. Now that we have an internet connection on the Pi, the final setup is to update the software packages already installed on the Pi. This can be done by opening a terminal, by clicking on the black monitor in the top left corner of the screen and typing the following commands:

```
sudo apt-get update
sudo apt-get upgrade
```

Each of these commands will take a few minutes to execute. The first updates the list of the available packages and the second updates each of the installed packages to the latest version.

Now that we have Raspbian setup on the Pi, we can move on to having a look at some of the tools we can use to write and execute Python scripts on the Pi.

The Python development tools

Now that the Pi is set up and running Raspbian, we can have a look at some of the tools we will use to develop Python scripts (small text files containing commands) and applications. Most of the time we will be using either the interactive Python terminal to execute the code line by line or the `python` executable to run full scripts and applications.

We will first look at the interactive terminal. First open a terminal by clicking on the black monitor icon in the top right corner of the desktop. This will open an LXTerminal window. In this window, type `python` and press *Enter*. This will start the interactive terminal as shown in the following screenshot:

From here we can type the Python code line by line; each line is executed as soon as it is typed, making this tool useful for quick testing and debugging (I also find that it makes a nice command line calculator). To demonstrate this, type in the following code and press *Enter*:

```
print "Hello, world!"
```

This will print the test `Hello, world!` on the line next to where you typed it in, as shown in the following screenshot:

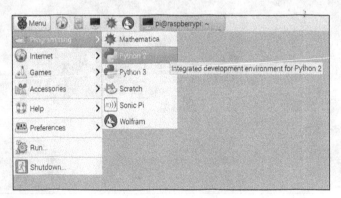

The `python` executable can also be used to run the existing Python script files (which have the `.py` file extension), which we will look at later in the chapter.

One alternative to the interactive terminal is the IDLE **Integrated Development Environment (IDE)** which can be used both as an interactive terminal and a source file editor, and provides syntax highlighting for the Python files. It can be found by selecting **Python 2** from the **Programming** submenu of the main menu on Raspbian, as shown in the following screenshot:

When first opened, it will be in the interactive terminal mode and can be used in the same way as the terminal ran from the command line, as shown in the following screenshot:

Python 2 versus Python 3

You will notice that there are two versions of Python installed by default on Raspbian: Python 2.7 and Python 3.1. Whilst the fundamentals of Python programming have not greatly changed between the two versions, there are notable differences that may prevent a code that was written for one version from working when executed with the interpreter for a different version.

For this reason, we will only use Python 2.7 in this book as this has the widest library support and is still the default Python version on many operating systems.

 More information of the differences between Python versions is available on the Python Wiki at `wiki.python.org/moin/Python2orPython3`.

Running some simple Python scripts

Now we will look at writing a Python script in a file and executing it. For this we will use IDLE as it will provide syntax highlighting on the code. However, any text editor (for example, LeafPad, GEdit, nano, vim) can be used to write the Python files.

1. First open IDLE and select **New Window** from the **File** menu, as shown in the following screenshot. This will open a new text editor window which will allow you to write and edit the script files.

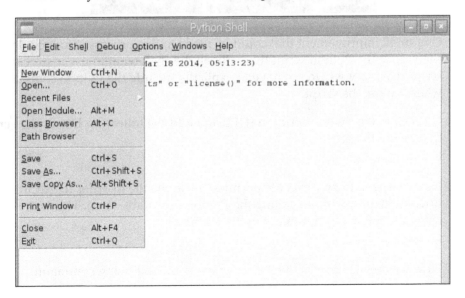

2. Now type the following code into the editor. This is a simple script that imports the `time` module and prints a string containing the current time to the terminal.

```
import time
print "The current time is: " + time.ctime()
```

 Keep in mind that the indentation level in Python is very important as this defines the scope that a line of code fits into. This will become clearer later on in the book when we start writing more complex codes.

3. Save the file as `time.py` in the home directory by selecting **Save** from the **File** menu.

Now that the script is saved, we can execute it using the Python executable at the command line.

4. Open a terminal and enter the following command to execute the Python script:

```
python time.py
```

This will give the following output to the terminal:

```
pi@raspberrypi ~ $ python time.py
The current time is: Sat May  2 10:41:28 2015
pi@raspberrypi ~ $
```

One small improvement that could be made to this process is to include a shebang in the Python script that will tell the shell what to use to execute the script. This way we do not have to explicitly include the Python command when we run the script.

5. Go back to the Python script in IDLE and add the following line as the very first line in the file:

```
#!/usr/bin/env python
```

6. Next, we need to give execute permissions to the file in order to execute it directly (that is, without calling the Python executable first). This is done using the following command in the terminal:

```
chmod a+x time.py
```

7. Now we are able to execute the script using the following command:

```
./time.py
```

This gives the following output on the terminal:

```
pi@raspberrypi ~ $ chmod a+x time.py
pi@raspberrypi ~ $ ./time.py
The current time is: Sat May  2 10:42:07 2015
pi@raspberrypi ~ $ □
```

Summary

In this chapter, we looked at getting the Pi set up and running using the Raspbian operating system, and went through the Python development tools and the differences between the Python versions.

We also looked at our first snippets of Python code and the different ways that Python can be executed.

In the next chapter, we will focus more on the fundamentals of Python programming when we look at control flow operations, multiple data types, and the operations they support.

2
Understanding Control Flow and Data Types

Now that we are able to run Python code, we will take a look at some of the ways in which we can store data and control the flow of execution through the Python code.

In this chapter, we will cover:

- The basics of data types in Python
- Using the `math` module for operations on numerical types
- Using the `tring` module for string manipulation

As mentioned earlier, all the code used in this chapter is written for Python 2.7, and is able to be executed on any Python 2.7 interpreter.

Data in Python

Before jumping to the various data types that are available in Python, it is worth noting that Python is a strong dynamically typed programming language, which means both that:

- Once a variable (a unit of stored data in a program) has been given a value, its type is set and will not change until the variable is assigned a value of a different type (strong)
- A variable can hold a value of any type as the type is given by the value, not the variable itself (dynamic)

This is best explained with an example that can be executed from the interactive console, assuming we have a variable representing a string:

```
flan = "flan"
```

We can query the value held by the variable and the type using the following code (note that this will only work on an interactive console as return values are automatically printed to the terminal):

```
flan
type(flan)
```

As the following output shows, the variable is of type `str` which represents a string in Python:

```
>>> flan = "flan"
>>> flan
'flan'
>>> type(flan)
<type 'str'>
>>>
```

We can now reassign the variable to a new numerical value and check the type as done earlier:

```
flan = 495
flan
type(flan)
```

Now when we check the type, we see the type has changed to type `int`, the type used to store an integer value.

```
>>> flan = 495
>>> flan
495
>>> type(flan)
<type 'int'>
>>>
```

You can also use the `isinstance()` function to test if a variable holds a value of a given type, as demonstrated in the following image:

```
>>> flan = "flan"
>>> isinstance(flan, str)
True
>>> isinstance(flan, int)
False
>>>
```

Certain types can be converted by using the type name as a function, as shown in the following example:

```
flan = "495"
flan
type(flan)
flan_i = int(flan)
flan_i
type(flan_i)
```

As the output shows, this converts the original value of the `flan` variable to an integer based on the contents of the string:

```
>>> flan = "495"
>>> flan
'495'
>>> type(flan)
<type 'str'>
>>> flan_i = int(flan)
>>> flan_i
495
>>> type(flan_i)
<type 'int'>
>>>
```

Numerical types

Python has several different numerical types built in that allow you to represent integer, floating point, and complex numbers using the following types:

- `int`: The plain integer type, this has at least 32 bits of precision but is limited by the architecture of the system
- `long`: This behaves in the same way as `int` but has unlimited precision
- `float`: Floating point numbers
- `complex`: Complex numbers

There are a range of ways to define a numerical value in Python. Typically, this can be done by typing the standard representation of a number as shown in the following example:

```
a = 42
type(a)
b = 0.009
type(b)
c = 10000000000
type(c)
```

```
d = 100L
type(d)
```

Following is the output of this code:

```
>>> a = 42
>>> type(a)
<type 'int'>
>>> b = 0.009
>>> type(b)
<type 'float'>
>>> c = 10000000000
>>> type(c)
<type 'long'>
>>> d = 100L
>>> type(d)
<type 'long'>
>>>
```

As the output shows, each numerical value is assigned a different type in Python:

- Since the value of a is less than the maximum precision of the system, int is used
- b uses float as its value is a decimal number
- c uses long as its value is greater than the maximum precision of the system
- Finally, d uses long as adding L to the end of an integer number explicitly makes it a long type

Since we have mentioned the maximum numerical precision of a particular system, we will quickly look at how we can actually find out what the value of this is. Python provides this value in the sys module (which is used to retrieve information about the host system).

```
import sys
sys.maxint
```

This returns the maximum value that can be held as an int, as shown in the following screenshot; anything larger will use the long type instead:

```
>>> import sys
>>> sys.maxint
2147483647
>>>
```

Integer types can also be defined using hexadecimal and binary notation using the `0x` and `0b` prefixes, as shown in the following example:

```
e = 0xFF
e
type(e)
f = 0b11111111
f
type(f)
```

As the following screenshot shows, both numbers evaluate to an integer with the value 255:

```
>>> e = 0xFF
>>> e
255
>>> type(e)
<type 'int'>
>>> f = 0b11111111
>>> f
255
>>> type(f)
<type 'int'>
>>>
```

Using this format for integer types will become more useful later when we start interacting with the GPIO expansion header on the Raspberry Pi.

Floating point and complex numbers also have their own syntax, based on the standard scientific syntax for their notation.

```
g = 2.75e-3
g
type(g)
h = (5+3j)
h
type(h)
```

Downloading the example code

You can download the example code files from your account at http://www.packtpub.com for all the Packt Publishing books you have purchased. If you purchased this book elsewhere, you can visit http://www.packtpub.com/support and register to have the files e-mailed directly to you.

This creates a floating point and complex number respectively, as shown in the following output:

```
>>> g = 2.75e-3
>>> g
0.00275
>>> type(g)
<type 'float'>
>>> h = (5+3j)
>>> h
(5+3j)
>>> type(h)
<type 'complex'>
>>>
```

It is also possible to create numerical types explicitly using the type name as a function, as shown in the following example. Doing this also allows you to convert between different numerical types and create numerical types by parsing strings.

```
a = int(4)
a
type(a)
b = int("4")
b
type(b)
c = long(4)
c
type(c)
d = int(5.9864)
d
type(d)
e = float(9)
e
type(e)
f = complex(3, 8)
f
type(f)
g = int("one")
```

The output from this previous example is shown in the following screenshot. Note that for the last variable (g), an exception was raised as there was no way to convert the string to an int type (we will cover exceptions in more detail later on in the chapter).

```
>>> a = int(4)
>>> a
4
>>> type(a)
<type 'int'>
>>> b = int("4")
>>> b
4
>>> type(b)
<type 'int'>
>>> c = long(4)
>>> c
4L
>>> type(c)
<type 'long'>
>>> d = int(5.9864)
>>> d
5
>>> type(d)
<type 'int'>
>>> f = complex(3, 8)
>>> f
(3+8j)
>>> type(f)
<type 'complex'>
>>> g = int("one")

Traceback (most recent call last):
  File "<pyshell#137>", line 1, in <module>
    g = int("one")
ValueError: invalid literal for int() with base 10: 'one'
>>>
```

Operations on numerical types

If you have ever used any other programming language then the numerical operators you will find in Python will not be greatly different. The main operators are listed as follows:

- `x + y`: Returns the value of the addition of x and y
- `x - y`: Returns the value of y subtracted from x
- `x * y`: Returns the product of x and y
- `x / y`: Returns the quotient of x and y
- `x // y`: Returns the integer quotient of x and y (integer division)
- `x % y`: Returns the remainder of `x // y` (modulo)
- `abs(x)`: Returns the absolute value of x (that is, removes the negative sign)

- `divmod(x, y)`: Returns `tuple` containing x `//` y and x `%` y (we will look at the `tuple` type in more detail in the next chapter)
- `x ** y` or `pow(x, y)`: Returns x to the power y

It is worth noting that with the exception of complex numbers, which do not work for integer division, module, and the `divmod()` operations, you can use any combination of numerical types with these functions.

Following is an example of these operations:

```
a = 49
b = 5
c = 6.5
d = 3e-9
e = 100L
a + b
a - b
a / b
a // b
a % b
c / d
e / a
div, rem = divmod(a, b)
div
rem
```

The output of this preceding code is shown next. You may wish to use the `type()` functions here to check the return type of each of the operations.

```
>>> a = 49
>>> b = 5
>>> c = 6.5
>>> d = 3e-9
>>> e = 100L
>>> a + b
54
>>> a - b
44
>>> a / b
9
>>> a // b
9
>>> a % b
4
>>> c / d
2166666666.6666665
>>> e / a
2L
>>> div, rem = divmod(a, b)
>>> div
9
>>> rem
4
>>>
```

One thing to note here is that despite the fact that 49/5 is actually 9.8, when we execute `49/5` in Python, the result will be 9. Because both operands are of type `int` only integer division was performed and hence the return value will effectively be the floored value (that is, the value with the decimal part subtracted) of the actual result.

It is also possible to perform certain operations directly on the left hand side value of the operation. In this case, the value held by the left hand side is modified and no value is returned. This is supported by the following operations:

- `+`, becomes a `+= b`
- `-`, becomes a `-= b`
- `*`, becomes a `*= b`
- `/`, becomes a `/= b`
- `//`, becomes a `//= b`
- `%`, becomes a `%= b`
- `**`, becomes a `**= b`

The following example demonstrates this format for the operators. Note that here you need to print out the output in order to see that the value is being changed.

```
a = 45
b = 5
a += b
a
a -= b
a
a *= b
a
a /= b
a
```

The output of this is shown in the following screenshot:

```
>>> a = 45
>>> b = 5
>>> a += b
>>> a
50
>>> a -= b
>>> a
45
>>> a *= b
>>> a
225
>>> a /= b
>>> a
45
>>>
```

 While the standard Python functions provide most numerical operations that you are likely to need, the SciPy package has a lot of tools that are better suited to working with large amounts of numerical data. Refer to www.scipy.org for more details.

String manipulation

The next topic we will look at is string storage and manipulation. As with numerical types, strings can be assigned using a **literal** (a value written exactly as it should be interpreted) as the right hand operand of the assignment operator =. You can also take a majority of any other type and convert it to a string using the str() function as shown in the following example:

```
a = "Hello, world!"
a
type(a)
b = complex(3, 6)
b
type(b)
c = str(b)
c
type(c)
```

The output of this is shown in the following screenshot:

```
>>> a = "Hello, world!"
>>> a
'Hello, world!'
>>> type(a)
<type 'str'>
>>> b = complex(3, 6)
>>> b
(3+6j)
>>> type(b)
<type 'complex'>
>>> c = str(b)
>>> c
'(3+6j)'
>>> type(c)
<type 'str'>
>>>
```

String functions

There are a large number of functions for performing manipulation and searching on a string object in Python. Here we will have a quick look at some of the more common and useful ones. The full list is available online at docs.python.org/2/library/stdtypes.html#string-methods.

Following is a list of the most common string manipulation functions and a quick example of how they are used:

- capitalize: This returns a copy of the string with the first character capitalized and the remaining characters in lower case. For example:

  ```
  "hello, world".capitalize()
  ```

  This example would return the string 'Hello, world', as shown in the following output:

  ```
  >>> "hello, world".capitalize()
  'Hello, world'
  >>>
  ```

- lower: This returns a copy of the string with all the characters converted to lower case. For example:

  ```
  "Hello World".lower()
  ```

This example would return the string `"hello world"` as shown in the following output:

```
>>> "Hello World".lower()
'hello world'
```

- `upper`: This returns a copy of the string with all the characters converted to upper case. For example:

```
"Hello World".upper()
```

This example would return the string `"HELLO WORLD"` as shown in the following output:

```
>>> "Hello World".upper()
'HELLO WORLD'
```

- `find`: This returns the first index in the string where a substring is found, or -1 if the substring is not found. Optionally, limits can also be provided to specify the search range. For example:

```
"The quick brown fox".find("brown")
"The quick brown fox".find("green")
"the quick brown fox jumps over the lazy dog".find
("the", 5)
```

The output of this example is shown in the following screenshot. Note how the second search failed and returned `-1`, and the third returned the index of the second `"the"` rather than the first as the search only began at the 5th character.

```
>>> "The quick brown fox".find("brown")
10
>>> "The quick brown fox".find("green")
-1
>>> "the quick brown fox jumps over the lazy dog".find("the", 5)
31
>>>
```

- `replace`: This replaces a given substring with a replacement string, optionally stopping after a given number of replacements have been done. For example:

```
"She sells seashells by the seashore".replace("sea",
"ocean")
"She sells seashells by the seashore".replace("sea",
"ocean", 1)
```

As the following screenshot shows, the first example replaces all occurrences of "sea" with "ocean"; in the second example, only the first occurrence was changed as a limit of 1 replacement was specified.

```
>>> "She sells seashells by the seashore".replace("sea", "ocean")
'She sells oceanshells by the oceanshore'
>>> "She sells seashells by the seashore".replace("sea", "ocean", 1)
'She sells oceanshells by the seashore'
>>>
```

- `strip`: This removes excess whitespace characters from the start and end of a string (leaving whitespace inside the string untouched) and returns the new string. For example:

```
"   Hello,    world  !   ".strip()
```

Here, the string "Hello,   world !" is returned as shown in the following output:

```
>>> "   Hello,    world  !   ".strip()
'Hello,    world  !'
>>>
```

- `split`: This splits a string on a given delimiter up to an optional maximum number of times returning a list of the new strings. If the delimiter is not found then a single string will be returned. For example:

```
"Eggs, Milk, Bread".split(", ")
"Eggs, Milk, Bread".split(", ", 1)
"Eggs, Milk, Bread".split("\t")
```

As the following screenshot of the output shows, the first example splits each of the items into its own string, the second stops after it has performed one split, and the third returns a single string as the delimiter (\t is the escape sequence for the *Tab* key) was not found in the string:

```
>>> "Eggs, Milk, Bread".split(", ")
['Eggs', 'Milk', 'Bread']
>>> "Eggs, Milk, Bread".split(", ", 1)
['Eggs', 'Milk, Bread']
>>> "Eggs, Milk, Bread".split("\t")
['Eggs, Milk, Bread']
>>>
```

- **in**: This determines if a string contains a given substring. For example:

```
"Bread" in "Eggs, Milk, Bread"
"Butter" in "Eggs, Milk, Bread"
```

Each expression evaluates to a **boolean** (a value that can either be true or false), as shown in the following output:

```
>>> "Bread" in "Eggs, Milk, Bread"
True
>>> "Butter" in "Eggs, Milk, Bread"
False
>>>
```

Note that a lot of these functions are called by adding the function to the end of the string itself. This is because in Python strings are what are known as **objects** (collections of data and functions that represent a part of a system). We will see this in more detail later on in the book.

String formatting

Python supports both the conventional style string formatting using the `%` identifier syntax (for example, `%.5d` is an integer with up to 5 leading zeros) which can be found in a lot of other programming languages, and Python's own (more powerful) string formatting mini-language.

Here we will only look at the conventional style formatting as it is usually good enough for the majority of uses and is much simpler to understand. The details for the Python formatting language can be found online at `docs.python.org/2/library/string.html#string-formatting`.

The conventional string formatting is done in Python using the syntax in the following example:

```
"%s is %d years old" % ("Alice", 23)
```

This returns the string `"Alice is 23 years old"`, as shown in the following output:

```
>>> "%s is %d years old" % ("Alice", 23)
'Alice is 23 years old'
>>>
```

There are several additional formatting options that can be used here to control how the string is formatted. The complete documentation can be found online at `docs.python.org/2/library/stdtypes.html#string-formatting-operations`.

A format string is made up of several sections as follows:

```
%[(name)][flags][minimum width][.precision][length]type
```

- `name`: This allows you to optionally specify the name of the key that is used to take the value from
- `flags`: This is used to control the type of conversion performed
- `minimum width`: This is used to pad out the value so that the string is a certain number of characters long
- `precision`: This is used to specify the precision of the numerical types
- `length`: This allows you to modify the length of the numerical types
- `type`: This is the character representing the data type of the parameter

Following is a list of the most common data types:

- `s`: String
- `i`: Integer number
- `f`: Floating point number

String templates

String templates are very similar to string formatting. However, they use customized $ marked substitutions that rely less on the type of the variable being used for the substitution.

Templates are available via the `Template` class in the `string` module.

The following is a simple example of how templates can be used to format multiple strings:

```
from string import Template
hello_template = Template("Hello $name, welcome to Python!")
hello_template.substitue(name="Alice")
hello_template.substitue(name="Marisa")
hello_template.substitue(name="Reimu")
```

This example gives the following output on the interactive terminal:

```
>>> from string import Template
>>> hello_template = Template("Hello $name, welcome to Python!")
>>> hello_template.substitute(name="Alice")
'Hello Alice, welcome to Python!'
>>> hello_template.substitute(name="Marisa")
'Hello Marisa, welcome to Python!'
>>> hello_template.substitute(name="Reimu")
'Hello Reimu, welcome to Python!'
>>>
```

It is worth noting that the type of the parameter passed to the substitute function is not really that important as it will be converted to a string in order to be substituted into the template string. The following is an example of this:

```
from string import Template
t = Template("The number is $number")
t.substitute(number="one")
t.substitute(number=42)
t.substitute(number=100L)
t.substitute(number=4e-3)
t.substitute(number=(3+6j))
```

In the following screenshot, you will see that the output of each substitution simply gives whatever the standard string representation of each number is:

```
>>> from string import Template
>>> t = Template("The number is $number")
>>> t.substitute(number="one")
'The number is one'
>>> t.substitute(number=42)
'The number is 42'
>>> t.substitute(number=100L)
'The number is 100'
>>> t.substitute(number=4e-3)
'The number is 0.004'
>>> t.substitute(number=(3+6j))
'The number is (3+6j)'
>>>
```

So far, we have just been using keyword arguments (by passing an argument to the substitute function by name) to provide the substitutions to the template. However, it is also possible to provide a dictionary containing the values (we will be covering dictionaries in more detail in the next chapter), as in the following example:

```
from string import Template
t = Template("$person_a says $something to $person_b")
```

```
info = {"person_a": "Marisa", "something": "hello", "person_b":
"Alice"}
t. substitute(info)
```

This is equivalent to providing the values as parameters to `substitute` and will provide the following output:

```
>>> t.safe_substitute(person_a="Mima")
'Mima says hello to $person_b'
>>> from string import Template
>>> t = Template("$person_a says $something to $person_b")
>>> info = {"person_a": "Marisa", "something": "hello", "person_b": "Alice"}
>>> t.substitute(info)
'Marisa says hello to Alice'
>>>
```

One issue with using `substitute` to perform the replacement is that an exception is raised if one of the substitution parameters is missing. Depending on the application, this may or may not be the desired behavior, but for cases where the call should not fail, there is the `safe_substitute` function which will never raise an exception. This is shown with the following example:

```
from string import Template
t = Template("$person_a says hello to $person_b")
t.substitute(person_a="Mima")
t.safe_substitute(person_a="Mima")
```

As shown in the following output, the first substitution fails as the `person_b` parameter is missing. However, when `safe_substitute` is used instead, the substitution completes but skips replacing the template parameter in the template string with anything.

```
>>> from string import Template
>>> t = Template("$person_a says hello to $person_b")
>>> t.substitute(person_a="Mima")

Traceback (most recent call last):
  File "<pyshell#2>", line 1, in <module>
    t.substitute(person_a="Mima")
  File "C:\Python27\lib\string.py", line 172, in substitute
    return self.pattern.sub(convert, self.template)
  File "C:\Python27\lib\string.py", line 162, in convert
    val = mapping[named]
KeyError: 'person_b'
>>> t.safe_substitute(person_a="Mima")
'Mima says hello to $person_b'
>>>
```

Control flow operators

If you have ever used any other programming language, you are probably familiar with the standard control flow operators `if`, `for`, and `while`, which are all present in Python and operate in a fairly similar way.

`if` and `while` can be used in a similar way as they would usually be with any Boolean expression, as shown in the following example. Since the interactive terminal is not fantastic at handling indentation, we will just run these examples as standard Python scripts.

```python
import random
if random.randint(1, 100) % 2 == 1:
    print "Win!"
else:
    print "Lose!"
times_lost = 0
while random.randint(1, 100) % 2 == 0:
    times_lost += 1
print "Win! (after %d losses)" % (times_lost)
```

As the following output shows, the execution in the first example is controlled solely by the random number generated in the `if` statement. In the second, the random number generation determines the amount of times a section of code will be executed whilst the overall control flow stays constant. To see the random execution of this script you may want to run this multiple times.

```
>>>
Lose!
Win! (after 2 losses)
>>>
```

You might have seen that in the previous example we also used the else statement to define what to do in the event that the Boolean expression evaluates to `False`. We can extend this by using the `elif` statement after an `if` statement to give more options. This functionality then becomes similar to the `switch` statements you may find in the other programming languages (which is not included in Python). The following example demonstrates the usage of `elif`:

```python
import random
number = random.randint(0, 3)
if number == 2:
    print "Big Win!"
elif number == 1:
```

```
        print "Small Win!"
    else:
        print "Lose!"
```

Here you can see that the `print` statement to be executed is chosen by the value of the `number` variable (which can only be between 0 and 2). Again, you may want to try running this code multiple times to see the random nature of the execution.

```
>>>
Lose!
>>> =======
>>>
Big Win!
>>> =======
>>>
Big Win!
>>> =======
>>>
Lose!
>>>
```

The `for` loops work slightly different in Python as they operate over objects called iterators and generators. Typically, all data storage containers will be iterable.

```
people = ["Sakuya", "Youmu", "Reisen"]
for person in people:
    print "Hello %s" % (person)
```

As shown in the following output, each of the values in the list is used as a value in the `for` loop. This makes it very easy to iterate over sets of data regardless of the data type.

```
>>>
Hello Sakuya
Hello Youmu
Hello Reisen
>>>
```

There are also several functions to create numerical ranges to iterate over. These functions are known as generators. The `range()` function allows you to use `for` in a similar integer indexed way as in the other programming languages, as shown in the following example:

```
for i in range(5):
    print i
for i in range(8, 12):
    print i
```

As the following output shows, the range function simply generates a list of numbers over the range supplied in the parameters which can be used to iterate over. This is equivalent to the standard integer indexed for loop iteration used in many other programming languages (C, for example).

```
>>>
0
1
2
3
4
8
9
10
11
>>>
```

Python also has the break operator which can be used to exit the current loop when called within one, as demonstrated in the following example:

```python
for i in range(2):
    for j in range(10):
        print "Starting %d.%d" % (i, j)
        if j > 5:
            break
        print "Finishing %d.%d" % (i, j)
```

As you can see from the following output, after the second iterator variable (j) reaches a value greater than 5, control exits the inner loop and continues in the outer loop:

```
>>>
Starting 0.0
Finishing 0.0
Starting 0.1
Finishing 0.1
Starting 0.2
Finishing 0.2
Starting 0.3
Finishing 0.3
Starting 0.4
Finishing 0.4
Starting 0.5
Finishing 0.5
Starting 0.6
Starting 1.0
Finishing 1.0
Starting 1.1
Finishing 1.1
Starting 1.2
Finishing 1.2
Starting 1.3
Finishing 1.3
Starting 1.4
Finishing 1.4
Starting 1.5
Finishing 1.5
Starting 1.6
>>>
```

The other common operator we can use in loops is `continue`. This allows us to skip the remaining sections of the loop and start at the beginning of the loop code with the next iterator value. This is best demonstrated with the following example:

```
for i in range(10):
    print "Starting #%d" % (i)
    if i % 2 == 1:
        continue
    print "Finishing #%d" % (i)
```

Here the second `print` statement is skipped for every odd number in the range, as shown in the following output:

```
>>>
Starting #0
Finishing #0
Starting #1
Starting #2
Finishing #2
Starting #3
Starting #4
Finishing #4
Starting #5
Starting #6
Finishing #6
Starting #7
Starting #8
Finishing #8
Starting #9
>>>
```

Using functions

The final topic we will cover in this chapter is that of separating code into functions, and how variables can be passed to and returned from them.

We will first start with a simple function that takes no arguments and does not return a value. The following example shows the basic syntax for a function in Python:

```
def say_hello():
    print "Hello!"
say_hello()
```

This example simply prints `Hello!` to the terminal, as shown in the following output:

```
>>>
Hello!
>>>
```

In the next example, we will introduce an argument which will be used in the string. As the example shows, all that is needed is the argument name unlike the other programming languages, which require a type.

```
def say_hello(person_name):
    print "Hello, %s!" % (person_name)
say_hello("Sanae")
```

 If you have a function that only operates on a specific type, you can still enforce arguments to take a specific type using the isinstance() function.

Here the string Hello, Sanae! is printed as shown in the following screenshot:

```
>>>
Hello, Sanae!
>>>
```

Like many other programming languages, Python allows you to set default values for arguments. This allows them to be omitted in the function call, as shown in this next example:

```
def say_hello(person_name="you"):
    print "Hello, %s!" % (person_name)
say_hello()
say_hello("Komachi")
```

The following output shows that the first call takes the default value for the person_ name argument and so prints the string Hello, you! In the second call, the value of the argument is provided in the call, so the printed string is Hello, Komachi!

```
>>>
Hello, you!
Hello, Komachi!
>>>
```

In this next example, we will use the return statement to return the string from the out function instead of printing it directly to the terminal. We will then print the return value of the function calls.

```
def say_hello(person_name="you"):
    return "Hello, %s!" % (person_name)
print say_hello()
print say_hello("Yuyuko")
```

As the following output shows, this script behaves in the same way as the previous example, but despite that fact, the structure of the code has changed:

```
>>>
Hello, you!
Hello, Yuyuko!
>>> |
```

Python has support for positional arguments which essentially means that instead of naming the arguments to a function, you will have access to a list of all the arguments (that have not already been named), as shown in the following example:

```
def say_hello(*args):
    for person in args:
        print "Hello, %s!" % (person)
say_hello()
say_hello("Sanae")
say_hello("Remilia", "Yuuka", "Orin")
```

Here we are taking `args` as a list of names passed to the function and iterating over them, as shown in the following screenshot. The asterix (*) is the syntax that tells Python that `args` is the list of the positional arguments. Once inside the function, `args` behaves just like a standard `list`.

```
>>>
Hello, Sanae!
Hello, Remilia!
Hello, Yuuka!
Hello, Orin!
>>> |
```

Python also supports what are called keyword arguments. These behave in a similar way as positional arguments, that is you define a single parameter in the function signature and can pass any number of values to it. However, they also require a name to be passed to the function when it is called, as shown in the following example:

```
def say_hello(*args, **kwargs):
    for person in args:
        greeting = kwargs.get("greeting", "Hello")
        print "%s, %s!" % (greeting, person)
say_hello()
say_hello("Tenshi")
say_hello("Eirin", "Keine", greeting="Good morning")
```

Here `kwargs` acts as a dictionary (`dict`) object and is identified as the keyword argument by the double asterix (`**`). When calling the function, keyword arguments are passed in key=value pairs and since there is no guarantee about what information will be passed, it is important to do proper checking before accessing a member of the dictionary (we will cover this in the next chapter).

The output of the preceding example is shown in the following screenshot:

```
>>>
Hello, Tenshi!
Good morning, Eirin!
Good morning, Keine!
>>>
```

Summary

In this chapter, we looked at the most common data types in Python, took an overview of their operations, and understood how control flow can be controlled within a Python script.

In the next chapter, we will look further into the container data types that can be used to hold multiple pieces of data. We will also take a look at IO and see how our Python programs can interact with the other data and devices on the system.

3
Working with
Data Structures and I/O

In this chapter, we will take a look at:

- The various data structures that are included in the standard Python types
- How they can be used to manage multiple sets of data in a Python application
- Reading and writing files to and from the disk to allow your applications to save their state or operate over data that already exists in a file on disk

Data structures

Data structures are containers that hold multiple variables, depending on the particular use case. There are multiple different data structures that can be used which we will now take a look at.

Lists

Lists are probably the most basic data structure; it is simply a list of variables that are numerically indexed by their position in the list.

Lists are most easily compared to array types that can be found in the other programming languages. However, they have the following properties that should be noted:

- **Zero indexed**: The numerical indices of lists start from 0 (as per the majority of other programming languages) rather than 1.
- **Dynamically sized**: Lists do not have a fixed size so they can grow to hold any number of elements.

- **Type agnostic**: Lists do not care about the type of the value that is stored within them (as the type is defined by the instance rather than the container). This means that there is no requirement for the values held in a list to be of the same type.

Creating lists

Lists can be created in multiple ways, the simplest of which is to explicitly list all of its elements, as shown in the following example:

```
l = ["apples", "milk", "bread", "eggs"]
print len(l)
print l
```

Here we are creating a list l containing four strings, and outputting the number of elements and the string representation of the entire list using the str function. The output of this can be seen in the following screenshot:

```
>>>
4
['apples', 'milk', 'bread', 'eggs']
>>>
```

Another way is to create an empty list and add items to it one by one. This is typically the way that items would be added if done based on execution of the program. A simple example of this is shown as follows:

```
breakfast = "french_toast"
l = []
if "toast" in breakfast:
    l.append("bread")
if breakfast == "french_toast":
    l.append("eggs")
elif breakfast == " cereal":
    l.append("milk")
    l.append("cereal")
print l
```

Here you can see that the elements in the list are determined programmatically by the value of the breakfast variable. As it is, this will create the list shown next but try changing breakfast to either "toast" or "cereal" to see the list output change.

```
>>>
['bread', 'eggs']
>>>
```

Another way to create a list is to use a generator. This is a piece of syntax that operates over sequence types (which include `str`, `unicode`, `list`, `tuple`, `buffer`, and `xrange`) and allows a simple way to either modify the elements of a sequence or include or exclude them based on a condition (or a combination of both).

The following example does exactly the same as the previous example, except that it chooses the ingredients for the breakfast from a list of all the ingredients, based on what is needed for the given breakfast (determined by the `needed_for` function):

```python
breakfast = "french_toast"
def needed_for(meal, item):
    if meal == "french_toast":
        return item in ["bread", "eggs"]
    if meal == "toast":
        return item in ["bread"]
    if meal == "cereal":
        return item in ["milk", "cereal"]
all_items = ["apples", "onions", "cereal", "milk", "bread", "bacon",
"eggs"]
l = [item for item in all_items if needed_for(breakfast, item)]
print l
```

As the following output shows, this works in the same way as the previous list example:

```
>>>
['bread', 'eggs']
>>> |
```

The following is an example of both modifying the values of a sequence (in this case a `str`) and conditionally excluding them.

It is an implementation of the Caesar cipher (`https://en.wikipedia.org/wiki/Caesar_cipher`), which is one of the simplest encryption algorithms that just replaces a letter with the one n places to the right of it, where n becomes the encryption key.

```python
import string
def caesar(letter, shift):
    letter = letter.upper()
    plain_idx = string.ascii_uppercase.index(letter)
    cipher_idx = (plain_idx + shift) % len(string.ascii_uppercase):
    cipher_letter = string.ascii_uppercase[cipher_idx]
    return cipher_letter
plain_text = "Hello, world!"
```

```
cipher_shift = 4
cipher = [caesar(char, cipher_shift) for char in plain_text if
char in string.ascii_letters]
print "".join(cipher)
```

The preceding code gives the following output. If you replace `plain_text` with this output and negate the `cipher_shift` value, then you will be able to decrypt the message back to **HelloWorld**, as shown in the following screenshot:

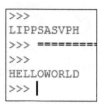

List operations

We will now have a quick look at some of the operations that can be done on lists. For this, we will use the following two lists:

```
items = ["milk", "bread", "eggs", "cheese", "crackers"]
more_items = ["honey", "jam", "bread"]
```

 Complete code for this example is provided in the `Lists_Operations.py` file supplied with this chapter.

- **Iteration**

```
for i in more_items:
    print i
```

Iteration is used to perform an operation (or a set of operations) using each value in the list.

- **String representation**

```
print str(items)
```

The `str` function is used to represent the list as a string. Typically, this is only used for logging and debugging.

- **Size**

```
print len(items)
```

The `len` function returns the number of items in the list.

- **Append full list**

  ```
  items.extend(more_items)
  print items
  ```

  The extend function allows you to append all the items from a second list to an existing list.

- **Get item**

  ```
  print items[2]
  print items[-3]
  ```

  Items can be retrieved from the list, given their index. A negative index is used to specify an index starting from the back of the list.

- **Slicing**

  ```
  print items[1:3]
  print items[::2]
  ```

  Slicing is used to generate a new list that is a subset of the existing one. The syntax is [min:max:step], where min and max define a range in the list and step defines the step between the indices in the range.

- **Existence test**

  ```
  print "milk" in items
  ```

  It tests to see if a given value is present in the list.

- **Insertion**

  ```
  items.append("tea")
  print items
  ```

  The append function adds a new value to the list.

- **Removal**

  ```
  items.remove("honey")
  print items
  ```

  The remove function removes an existing value from the list. If the value is not in the list then an exception will be raised.

- **Sort**

  ```
  items.sort()
  print items
  ```

  The sort function is used to sort a list using the natural ordering of the values it contains (that is, using the greater than and less than comparisons).

The output from the `Lists_Operations.py` script which runs all of these examples is shown in the following screenshot:

```
>>>
honey
jam
bread
['milk', 'bread', 'eggs', 'cheese', 'crackers']
5
['milk', 'bread', 'eggs', 'cheese', 'crackers', 'honey', 'jam', 'bread']
eggs
['bread', 'eggs']
['milk', 'eggs', 'crackers', 'jam']
True
2
['milk', 'bread', 'eggs', 'cheese', 'crackers', 'honey', 'jam', 'bread', 'tea']
['milk', 'bread', 'eggs', 'cheese', 'crackers', 'jam', 'bread', 'tea']
['bread', 'bread', 'cheese', 'crackers', 'eggs', 'jam', 'milk', 'tea']
>>>
```

Dictionaries

Dictionaries in Python represent a many to one mapping between values. Like lists, they can contain any hashable type (for example, `str`, `int`) as the key and any type as the value, and they do not have a fixed size.

They are commonly used to represent data where the fields are not typically fixed. For example, when parsing data in the **JavaScript Object Notation (JSON)** format, a tree of dictionaries is the most logical data container as it is a direct representation of the original data.

Creating dictionaries

Like lists, the contents of a dictionary can be given when creating it, as shown in the following example. Here the keys and values are separated by a colon (`:`) and each field by a comma (`,`).

```
d = {"name": "Keine", "Occupation": "Teacher"}
print len(d)
print d.keys()
print d
```

As shown in the following output, the `len` function returns the number of set fields in the dictionary. You will also notice the `keys` function which returns a list containing all the keys in the dictionary.

```
>>>
2
['name', 'Occupation']
{'name': 'Keine', 'Occupation': 'Teacher'}
>>>
```

Dictionaries also support setting the values of any key (or inserting new keys) using the syntax demonstrated in the following example:

```
d = dict()
d["name"] = "Keine"
d["occupation"] = "Teacher"
print d
print d["name"]
```

As the following output shows, this syntax can also be used to retrieve the value of any existing key in the dictionary:

```
>>>
{'name': 'Keine', 'occupation': 'Teacher'}
Keine
>>> |
```

Dictionary operations

We will now have a quick look at some of the operations that can be done on dictionaries. For this, we will use the following two sample dictionaries:

```
dict_a = {"eggs": 1.50, "milk": 1.2, "bacon": 2.99}
dict_b = {"bread": 2.20, "jam": 4.87}
dict_c = {}
```

 The complete code for this example is provided in the DIctionary_Operations.py file supplied with this chapter.

- **Number of keys:**

    ```
    print len(dict_a)
    ```

    This returns the number of key/value pairs in the dictionary.

- **Iteration:**

    ```
    for key, value in dict_b.iteritems():
        print "%s -> %f" % (key, value)
    ```

    This iterates over the key/value pairs in the dictionary.

- **Set key/value:**

```
dict_c["honey"] = 5.32
print dict_c
```

This sets a key to a given value, inserting the key if it does not already exist.

- **Get value:**

```
print dict_a["bacon"]
```

This returns the value associated with a given key. If the key does not exist then an exception will be raised.

- **Get value using a default value:**

```
print dict_b.get("bacon", 6.0)
```

This returns the value associated with a given key. If the key does not exist then the default value will be returned (6.0 in this case).

- **Remove a key/value pair:**

```
del dict_a["bacon"]
print dict_a
```

This removes a key/value pair from the dictionary.

- **Test if a key is in a dictionary:**

```
print "bacon" in dict_a
```

This tests to see if a given key is present in the dictionary.

- **List keys and values:**

```
print dict_a.items()
print dict_a.keys()
print dict_a.values()
```

This returns a list of key value pairs as tuples, a list of keys, and a list of values.

- **Update dictionary from another:**

```
dict_c.update(dict_b)
print dict_c
```

This copies the key/value pairs from dict_b to dict_c, overwriting the existing keys where necessary.

The output from the `Dictionary_Operations.py` script which runs all of these examples is shown in the following screenshot:

```
>>>
{'eggs': 1.5, 'bacon': 2.99, 'milk': 1.2}
{'jam': 4.87, 'bread': 2.2}
{}
3
jam -> 4.870000
bread -> 2.200000
{'honey': 5.32}
2.99
None
6.0
{'eggs': 1.5, 'milk': 1.2}
False
[('eggs', 1.5), ('milk', 1.2)]
['eggs', 'milk']
[1.5, 1.2]
{'honey': 5.32, 'jam': 4.87, 'bread': 2.2}
>>>
```

Sets

The `set` type in Python represents logical sets of values and as such supports the entire standard set logic and arithmetic operations.

The following example shows how sets can be created. The two main options for this are either creating an empty set as in the first example, or creating a set using the elements from an iterable storage type (such as `list`).

```
empty_set = set()
print len(empty_set)
print empty_set
values = range(0, 10, 2)
value_set = set(values)
print len(value_set)
print value_set
```

This first creates an empty set, then creates a set using the values generated by the `range` function and returns the contents of each as shown in the following screenshot:

```
>>>
0
set([])
5
set([0, 8, 2, 4, 6])
>>>
```

Set operations

We will now take a look at the operations that can be performed on sets. Most of these are just what you would expect following set algebra.

In this next example, we will use the following sample sets:

```
set_a = set(range(0, 10, 2))
set_b = set(range(5, 10))
set_c = set(range(5, 15))
```

 The complete code for this example is provided in the Sets_Operations.py file supplied with this chapter.

- **Number of members:**

  ```
  print len(set_a)
  ```

  This returns the number of members in a set.

- **Membership test:**

  ```
  print 6 in set_a
  ```

  This tests to see if a given value is a member of a set.

- **Disjoint test:**

  ```
  print set_b.isdisjoint(set_a)
  ```

  This tests to see if two sets are disjoint, that is, if the two sets have no common members.

- **Subset and superset test:**

  ```
  print set_b <= set_c
  print set_c >= set_b
  ```

  This tests if a set is a subset or superset of another set. Here the first line tests if set_b is a subset of set_c and the second line tests if set_c is a superset of set_b.

- **Union:**

  ```
  print set_a | set_b
  ```

  It returns the union of two sets, that is, a set containing all the members of both operand sets.

- **Intersection:**

  ```
  print set_a & set_b
  ```

  This returns the intersection of two sets, that is, the common members of both the sets.

- **Difference:**

  ```
  print set_a - set_b
  ```

  This returns a set containing members of the first set that are not in the second.

- **Symmetric Difference:**

  ```
  print set_a ^ set_b
  ```

  This returns the difference of both the sets, that is, the members that only appear in one of the two sets.

The output from the `Sets_Operations.py` script which runs all of these examples is shown in the following screenshot:

```
>>>
set([0, 8, 2, 4, 6])
set([8, 9, 5, 6, 7])
set([5, 6, 7, 8, 9, 10, 11, 12, 13, 14])
5
True
False
True
True
set([0, 2, 4, 5, 6, 7, 8, 9])
set([8, 6])
set([0, 2, 4])
set([0, 2, 4, 5, 7, 9])
>>> |
```

Frozen sets

There is also a `frozenset` type which behaves in the same way as a set, except that it is immutable, meaning that once it is created the value cannot be changed. This is shown in the following example where an attempt to add a value to `frozenset` is made:

```
values = range(0, 10, 2)
value_set = frozenset(values)
print value_set
value_set.add(20)
```

As shown in the following screenshot, the final line raises an exception as the add operation is not supported for the `frozenset` type:

```
>>>
frozenset([0, 8, 2, 4, 6])

Traceback (most recent call last):
  File "C:\Users\Dan\GettingStartedWithPythonAndRaspberryPi\Chapter03\Sets_Froze
n.py", line 9, in <module>
    value_set.add(20)
AttributeError: 'frozenset' object has no attribute 'add'
>>> 
```

Tuples

Tuples are very simple data structures. They are essentially lists that once created cannot be modified and do not have as wide of a selection of operations. They are commonly used for returning more than one value from a function.

A simple example of their usage is shown as follows:

```
t = ("Hello", 42, 42, "#")
for i in t:
    print i
print str(t)
print len(t)
print t[0]
print t[-2]
print t[1:3]
print t.count(42)
print t.index("#")
```

This shows the range of operations supported by tuples. This is essentially the standard data structure operators including `len`, iteration, and index access using `[]`. The output of this is shown in the following screenshot:

```
>>>
Hello
42
42
#
('Hello', 42, 42, '#')
4
Hello
42
(42, '#')
2
3
>>> 
```

Input/output

We will now take a look at some of the ways we can access the files and directories on the filesystem and create, modify, and read the files. Here we will look at using Python's file objects which are documented in full at `https://docs.python.org/2/library/stdtypes.html#bltin-file-objects`.

While this will suffice for simple files, there is a good selection of free libraries available online that take a lot of work out of creating and parsing the more complex files such as XML, JSON, and MIDI.

The os.path module

The `os.path` module contains various functions for performing manipulation of path names specific to the host operating system. This goes hand in hand with the file objects for accessing the files and directories on the filesystem, and helps to ensure that code can be used on any platform by handing all of the platform dependent and specific tasks for you (for example, the differences in file paths on Windows and Linux).

The following example demonstrates the most commonly used functions from this module. However, we first need to setup some paths to be used with the test script and create a sample file using the following code (where ~ denotes the home directory):

```
import os.path
homedir = os.path.expanduser("~")
filename_in_homedir = os.path.expanduser("~/SampleFile.txt")
with open(filename_in_homedir, "w") as f:
    f.write("test\n")
```

 The complete code for this example is provided in the `os_path.py` file supplied with this chapter.

The following are the most common and useful functions from `os.path`:

- abspath

  `print os.path.abspath("SampleFile.txt")`

  This returns an absolute path given a relative path. In this case, the absolute path will be for a file named `SampleFile.txt` in whatever directory the script was executed from.

- basename

  `print os.path.basename(filename_in_homedir)`

This returns the basename of the file that the path points to. The base name is the filename with the extension.

- `exists`

```
print os.path.exists(filename_in_homedir)
```

This returns a Boolean indicating if the path exists on the file system. This could mean the path is either a file or directory of symbolic link.

- `getsize`

```
print os.path.getsize(filename_in_homedir)
```

This returns the size in bytes of a file or directory.

- `isfile`

```
print os.path.isfile(filename_in_homedir)
```

This returns a Boolean indicating whether the path points to an existing file.

- `isdir`

```
print os.path.isdir(homedir)
```

This returns a Boolean indicating whether the path points to an existing directory.

- `islink`

```
print os.path.islink(homedir)
```

This returns a Boolean indicating whether the path points to an existing symbolic link.

- `expanduser`

```
print os.path.expanduser("~/SampleFile.txt")
```

This expands markers at the start of the path that denote the user's home directory, namely ~ and ~user.

- `join`

```
print os.path.join(homedir, "SampleFile.txt")
```

This joins two paths together, automatically inserting slashes as required.

- `split`

```
print os.path.split(filename_in_homedir)
```

This splits a path into the path and basename.

- `splitext`

  ```
  print os.path.splitext(filename_in_homedir)
  ```

  This splits a path into the path with filename and the file extension.

The output from the `os_path.py` script which runs all of these examples is shown in the following screenshot:

```
>>>
C:\Users\Dan\GettingStartedWithPythonAndRaspberryPi\Chapter03\SampleFile.txt
SampleFile.txt
True
6
True
True
False
C:\Users\Dan/SampleFile.txt
C:\Users\Dan\SampleFile.txt
('C:\\Users\\Dan', 'SampleFile.txt')
('C:\\Users\\Dan/SampleFile', '.txt')
>>> |
```

Reading and writing files

Now that we can query the filesystem and manipulate the file paths using the `os.path` module, we can look at accessing and writing files. In the following example, we will create a sample file in the home directory, write some test to it, and read it back.

The following first block of code simply imports the `os.path` module, and defines the file we are writing to and the text we are going to write:

```
import os.path
filename = os.path.expanduser("~/SampleFile.txt")
text = "The quick, brown fox jumps, over the, lazy dog"
```

Now we will open the file for writing using the `open` function. Here the first parameter is the filename and the second is the mode in which it will be opened. The possible options here are:

- `r`: Reading only (the default option when the second parameter is omitted)

- `w`: Writing (any file by the same name will be overwritten)

- `a`: Appending (appending to the existing file of the same name, otherwise create a new file)

- `r+`: Reading and writing

We then use the `writelines` function to write a list of strings to the file, as shown next:

```
with open(filename, "a") as f:
    lines = [l + "\n" for l in text.split(",")]
    f.writelines(lines)
```

Next, we will reopen the file in read only mode and print out its contents. Here we are using the `enumerate` function which adds a numerical index to an iterator:

```
with open(filename) as f:
    for idx, line in enumerate(f):
        print "%.2d: %s" % (idx, line.strip())
```

This results in the contents of the file being printed line by line alongside the line number, as shown in the following screenshot. Note that since we open the file in the append mode, running the script multiple times will add more duplicate lines to the file.

```
>>>
00: test
01: The quick
02: brown fox jumps
03: over the
04: lazy dog
>>> =================
>>>
00: test
01: The quick
02: brown fox jumps
03: over the
04: lazy dog
05: The quick
06: brown fox jumps
07: over the
08: lazy dog
>>> |
```

Summary

In this chapter, we looked at storing data sets in Python using the container types and how we can perform operations over an entire data set using the container operations as well as accessing files saved on the disk as plain text.

In the next chapter, we will learn about the **Object Oriented Programming (OOP)** paradigm, how this differs from the functional programming style we have been doing so far, and in what cases it should be used.

4
Understanding Object-oriented Programming and Threading

In this chapter, we will look at how **object-oriented programming** (**OOP**) can be done using Python, how code can be arranged into modules, and how these modules can be used in scripts.

We will also have a quick look at how multithreading can be used within a Python script in order to perform multiple operations simultaneously within the program.

In this chapter, we will cover the following topics:

- Object-oriented programming
- Classes in Python
- Threading

Object-oriented programming

Object-oriented programming is a paradigm in which the program is structured around several objects rather than actions or functionality. The main difference is that in the procedural programming type that we have been using so far in the book, the focus is on the processing that is being carried out, whereas in object-oriented programming, the focus is on the data being processed.

To demonstrate this, we will write a simple module that provides an interface similar to a conventional calculator, that is, input in the form of a series of numerical values and operations.

The structure for this module is shown in the following **Unified Modeling Language (UML)** (www.uml.org) diagram:

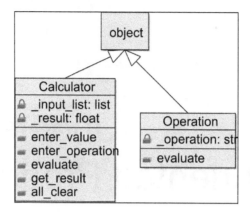

Here each block represents a class, with the second square representing the member variables of the class and the bottom representing the functions.

An arrow indicates that a class inherits from the class it points to. This essentially means that the class inherits all of the parent class's functionality.

Before we start implementing this, it is important to get an idea of the file structure of the module. The structure required is shown in the following screenshot:

```
dan@dannixon-envy-ubuntu ~/calc_demo> tree
.
├── calculator
│   ├── Calculator.py
│   ├── __init__.py
│   └── Operation.py
└── do_calculation.py

1 directory, 4 files
```

This preceding screenshot was created with the tree utility, which can be installed using the following:

```
sudo apt-get install tree
```

 Note that __init__.py is just an empty file; it is, however, required to signify that the calculator directory is a Python module.

Classes in Python

We will now look at how we create classes in Python in our `calculator` module.

Operation.py

First, we will create the `Operation` class. It is used to represent a single operation that can be performed by the `Calculator` class. Here, we are inheriting from the `object` class, which is the base class from which all the objects inherit in Python.

```
class Operation(object):
    _operation = None
```

The `__init__` function is the constructor of the class. It is called when a new instance of a class is created. Here, we will use it to validate the function that is provided by a parameter and store it in the class.

```
    def __init__(self, name):
        if name not in ["add", "subtract", "multiply", "divide"]:
            raise ValueError("%s is not a valid operation" %
(name))
        self._operation = name
```

Methods in the Python classes are required to take a parameter typically named `self`. This parameter is the instance of the class that the function was called on, and it must be used when calling the other class functions or accessing the member variables. Here, we use this when accessing the _operation member variable:

```
    def evaluate(self, a, b):
        if self._operation == "add":
            return a + b
        elif self._operation == "subtract":
            return a - b
        elif self._operation == "multiply":
            return a * b
        elif self._operation == "divide":
            return a / b
```

Calculator.py

Now, we will create the `Calculator` class, which will contain the actual logic for calling the operations on the values provided.

As we will be using the `Operation` class, we first need to import it, as shown next:

```
from Operation import Operation

class Calculator(object):
    _input_list = list()
    _result = 0.0
```

The following two functions are used to add values and operations to the list of inputs to the calculator (stored in the `_input_list` member variable):

```
def enter_value(self, value):
    if len(self._input_list) > 0 and not
isinstance(self._input_list[-1], Operation):
        raise RuntimeError("Must enter an operation next")
    self._input_list.append(float(value))

def enter_operation(self, operation_name):
    if len(self._input_list) == 0 or
isinstance(self._input_list[-1], Operation):
        raise RuntimeError("Must enter a value next")
    self._input_list.append(Operation(operation_name))
```

The `evaluate` function is used to iterate through `_input_list` and perform operations on the values using the `Operation` class.

```
def evaluate(self):
    self._result = self._input_list[0]
    for idx in range(1, len(self._input_list), 2):
        operation = self._input_list[idx]
        next_value = self._input_list[idx + 1]
        self._result = operation.evaluate(self._result,
next_value)
    return self._result
```

Since the `_result` member variable is marked to be private to the class (that is, it should only be accessed and written to by the class and its subclasses), we will add a function to return its value.

```
def get_result(self):
    return self._result
```

Unlike other languages (such as C++), Python does not enforce privacy on the member variables and the class functions. However, the code conventions state that any function or variable starting with an underscore (_) is to be treated as private, and any modifications to them may cause unexpected behavior from the class.

The `all_clear` function is used to simply reset the result and the inputs to the calculator.

```
def all_clear(self):
    self._input_list = list()
    self._result = 0.0
```

Using the module

Now that the files for the module have been created, we can start writing a simple script that will make use of the module. First, we must import the class from the module, as shown next:

```
from calculator.Calculator import Calculator
```

Now we can use the `Calculator` class that we imported to perform some test operations, as follows:

```
c = Calculator()
c.enter_value(1)
c.enter_operation("add")
c.enter_value(9)
c.enter_operation("multiply")
c.enter_value(5)
c.enter_operation("divide")
c.enter_value(20)
print c.evaluate()
```

When executed, the script output the result of the calculation, as shown in the following screenshot:

The complete code for this example is provided in the do_calculation.py file and the calculator directory supplied with this chapter.

Inheritance

To better demonstrate the possible uses for inheritance, we will create a simple example showing how it can help to remove code duplication in a larger application. This sample script is a simple calculator that is designed for expanding the number of operations it can support; the structure of which is shown in the following UML diagram:

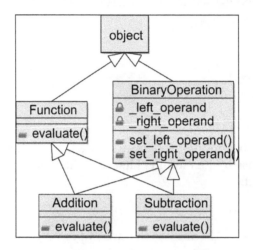

First, we will create the **Function** class that provides an interface for any subclass that inherits from it. Since Python can not explicitly state that a function must be overridden in a subclass, we will have the evaluate function raise NotImplementedError if it is called on a class that did not override it. This is used to indicate to the code that called the function that an error has occurred, and is done using the raise function.

```
class Function(object):
    def evaluate(self):
        raise NotImplementedError();
```

Next, we will create the BinaryOperation abstract class that will provide the functionality for setting and holding the operands for the operation.

```
class BinaryOperation(object):
    _left_operand = 0.0
    _right_operand = 0.0

    def set_left_operand(self, value):
        if not isinstance(value, float):
            raise ValueError("Value must be a float")
        self._left_operand = value
```

```
def set_right_operand(self, value):
    if not isinstance(value, float):
        raise ValueError("Value must be a float")
    self._right_operand = value
```

Next, we will create two operations that inherit from both `Function` and `BinaryOperation`. This will ensure that the new classes will have the `evaluate` function (if not, an informative error message will be generated) and will have access to the left and right operand member variables defined in the `BinaryOperation` class.

```
class Addition(Function, BinaryOperation):
    def evaluate(self):
        return self._left_operand + self._right_operand

class Subtraction(Function, BinaryOperation):
    def evaluate(self):
        return self._left_operand - self._right_operand
```

Next, we will write a simple script that demonstrates the usage of the two new classes.

```
add = Addition()
add.set_left_operand(5.0)
add.set_right_operand(10.0)
print add.evaluate()

sub = Subtraction()
sub.set_left_operand(50.0)
sub.set_right_operand(23.0)
print sub.evaluate()
```

When executed, this script should print the output of these two calculations, as shown in the following screenshot:

 The complete code for this example is provided in the `Inheritance.py` file supplied with this chapter.

Threading

Multithreading allows an application to have multiple flows of control that are executed simultaneously. On the Raspberry Pi, this can be useful in applications that need to monitor the **General Purpose Input and Output (GPIO)** pins to react to the changes in switch and sensor states.

Multithreading is a large subject that can take a long time to cover completely, hence only a couple of the Python classes in the threading module will be covered here. However, the full documentation for this module is available at https://docs.python.org/2/library/threading.html.

First, we will import the required modules for the functionality that we will be using and will set up the default logger so that we can see the process ID when a log is written to it. You don't need to worry about this now, as we will be going over the logging framework in Python in a later chapter.

```
import logging
import threading
import time
logging.basicConfig(level=logging.INFO,
                    format="%(asctime)s (T:%(thread)d):-
%(message)s")
```

Next, we will create a new class that inherits from the Thread class. This includes all the functionality to have the processing in the run function be performed on a new thread. In the constructor, we will also take the arguments passed to the class and store them to be used when the thread runs.

```
class MessagePrinter(threading.Thread):
    def __init__(self, *args, **kwargs):
        threading.Thread.__init__(self)
        self._args = args
        self._kwargs = kwargs
        self._lock = kwargs.get("lock", None)
    def run(self):
        for message in self._args:
            logging.info(message)
            time.sleep(self._kwargs.get("delay", 1.0))
```

Here, the `run` function will log each of the messages passed to the class as a positional argument, with a delay between them defined by the `delay` keyword argument.

Next, we will create two instances of the `MessagePrinter` class with different messages and delays, as can be seen next:

```
mp1 = MessagePrinter("Hello", "Good day!")
mp2 = MessagePrinter("A", "B", "C", delay=3)
```

To actually execute the `run` function, we call `start` on the class which will call the `run` function in a new child thread.

```
mp1.start()
mp2.start()
```

Since we now have two threads that will be running for a longer duration than the main thread (that is, the one that runs the entire script), we need to join the two child threads so that the main thread will have to wait for both of them to exit before it can exit.

```
mp1.join()
mp2.join()
```

When the script is run, you should see something similar to the following output. Note that the process IDs match the messages logged by each of the `MessagePrinter` classes.

```
>>>
2015-05-25 15:01:22,693 (T:8320):- Hello
2015-05-25 15:01:22,693 (T:4748):- A
2015-05-25 15:01:23,709 (T:8320):- Good day!
2015-05-25 15:01:25,720 (T:4748):- B
2015-05-25 15:01:28,795 (T:4748):- C
>>> |
```

The complete code for this example is provided in the `Threading.py` file supplied with this chapter.

Locks

An important concept in multithreading is the idea of a lock. It is used to prevent multiple threads from modifying the same data simultaneously, which can otherwise lead to data corruption.

A lock is said to have an owner (typically, a thread), and while a thread has ownership of a lock, it is allowed to write to data that is shared between multiple threads. When another thread requires a write access to some data, it must request ownership of the lock. If the lock has no owner, then the requesting thread is granted the ownership immediately; otherwise, the requesting thread must wait for the current owner to release its ownership on the lock before it can take ownership of it.

Whilst locks are typically used to protect data, they can also be used with input/output devices, including the standard output stream used by the print function, as shown in the following example (which is largely the same as the preceding example but does not use the logging framework):

```python
import logging
import threading
import time
class MessagePrinter(threading.Thread):
    def __init__(self, *args, **kwargs):
        threading.Thread.__init__(self)
        self._args = args
        self._kwargs = kwargs
        self._lock = kwargs.get("lock", None)
    def run(self):
        for message in self._args:
            if self._lock:
                self._lock.acquire()
            print message
            if self._lock:
                self._lock.release()
            time.sleep(self._kwargs.get("delay", 1.0))
lock = None
mp1 = MessagePrinter("Hello", "Good day!", lock=lock)
mp2 = MessagePrinter("A", "B", "C", delay=3, lock=lock)
mp1.start()
mp2.start()
mp1.join()
mp2.join()
```

Since we have the `lock` variable set to `None` in the preceding example, the script will make calls to the `print` function without any regard for other threads that may also be using the `print` function. As can be seen in the following output, this causes minor defects in the output that is printed to the terminal, since the first message on both the threads was printed simultaneously:

If instead, we replace the `lock` variable with an instance of a `Lock` object, then `MessagePrinter` will only make calls to the `print` function when it has ownership of the lock.

```
lock = threading.Lock()
```

Now that all the `MessagePrinter` instances share the same lock object, they will never print messages simultaneously. This can be seen in the following output which is correctly formatted:

The complete code for this example is provided in the `Threading_Locks.py` file supplied with this chapter.

Summary

In this chapter, we looked at the object-oriented programming paradigm and how it can benefit applications, and the way that classes can be combined into modules and used in other scripts.

We also had a brief introduction to multithreading and the best practices for ensuring data validity between the threads that access shared data.

In the next chapter, we will have a look at the `setuptools` utility and see how it can be used to package the Python code for distribution to multiple systems, and how it can help manage dependencies on the other libraries.

5

Packaging Code with setuptools

In this chapter, we will look at the ways we can use third-party libraries in our Python code and how we can package our own Python modules ready for distribution. The distribution can be done in a variety of ways including via the popular pip repository, which we will take a quick look at.

The following topics will be covered in this chapter:

- Using packages in your Python code
- Packaging your own Python modules

Using packages in your Python code

We will first have a look at the ways in which third party code and libraries can be downloaded, installed, and included in the Python scripts and application we write.

Importing modules

As we have already seen in several of the examples used so far, Python libraries (modules) are used in code by importing them using the `import` statement. However, so far, we have only been importing the entire modules. For example, `import threading` imports the entire `threading` module and to use, say, the `Thread` class, you would have to specify it as `threading.Thread`.

Python also allows you to import single classes, and even functions, using a slightly modified syntax, as shown next:

```
from threading import Thread
from time import time
```

This preceding code imports just the `Thread` class and the `time` function from the `threading` and `time` modules respectively. Now when you want to use either within the rest of the file, you would only need to specify either `Thread` or `time`, rather than `threading.Thread` or `time.time`.

It is also possible to specify multiple items to be imported from a single module using the following syntax. Note that the brackets are not required in this case. However, the use of brackets allows the import statement to span multiple lines if required (this is usually done for clarity if a line should exceed a certain number of characters, typically 80).

```
from time import (time, sleep)
```

Installing modules manually

So far, we have only used packages that are included with Python by default; however, installing third party packages is a simple process as well.

As an example, we will install and demonstrate the `PyDub` library, which provides an interface to allow simple audio modification and processing. This library is hosted on GitHub (`https://github.com/jiaaro/pydub`), so we can simply use Git to obtain a copy of the source code. The process after this remains the same for any packaged Python source code. Following are the steps to manually install it:

1. We will install the `git` client, download a copy of the source code to the `pydub` directory, and change into that directory using the following commands:

    ```
    sudo apt-get install git
    git clone https://github.com/jiaaro/pydub.git pydub
    cd pydub
    ```

     Git (`git-scm.com`) is an open source version control system that is commonly used to manage the open source projects.

2. Next, we will use the `setup.py` script to install the `PyDub` library using the following command:

    ```
    sudo python setup.py install
    ```

This command should give output similar to the following screenshot:

```
byte-compiling build/bdist.linux-x86_64/egg/pydub/silence.py to silence.pyc
byte-compiling build/bdist.linux-x86_64/egg/pydub/__init__.py to __init__.pyc
byte-compiling build/bdist.linux-x86_64/egg/pydub/generators.py to generators.pyc
creating build/bdist.linux-x86_64/egg/EGG-INFO
copying pydub.egg-info/PKG-INFO -> build/bdist.linux-x86_64/egg/EGG-INFO
copying pydub.egg-info/SOURCES.txt -> build/bdist.linux-x86_64/egg/EGG-INFO
copying pydub.egg-info/dependency_links.txt -> build/bdist.linux-x86_64/egg/EGG-INFO
copying pydub.egg-info/top_level.txt -> build/bdist.linux-x86_64/egg/EGG-INFO
zip_safe flag not set; analyzing archive contents...
creating dist
creating 'dist/pydub-0.11.1-py2.7.egg' and adding 'build/bdist.linux-x86_64/egg' to it
removing 'build/bdist.linux-x86_64/egg' (and everything under it)
Processing pydub-0.11.1-py2.7.egg
Copying pydub-0.11.1-py2.7.egg to /usr/local/lib/python2.7/dist-packages
Adding pydub 0.11.1 to easy-install.pth file

Installed /usr/local/lib/python2.7/dist-packages/pydub-0.11.1-py2.7.egg
Processing dependencies for pydub==0.11.1
Finished processing dependencies for pydub==0.11.1
dan@dannixon-envy-ubuntu ~/pydub (master=)> 
```

Before we can use the PyDub library, we must also install `ffmpec` (a media transcoding library and utility). This can be done using the following command:

```
sudo apt-get install ffmpeg
```

Once the library is installed, we can use it in a sample Python script, such as the one shown next. This does some simple audio synthesis and manipulation using PyDubs auto segment class and the `Pulse` generator.

```
from pydub.generators import Pulse

audio = Pulse(440, duty_cycle=0.6).to_audio_segment() * 10
faded = audio.fade_in(2500).fade_out(5000)
faded.export("test_audio.mp3", format="mp3")
```

The preceding script will not give any visual output but you will see that there is an mp3 file that is created by it. This file should contain a tone played for 10 seconds with a fade in and out, as described in the Python script.

```
dan@dannixon-envy-ubuntu ~/G/Chapter05 (book_release=)> python pydub_sample.py
dan@dannixon-envy-ubuntu ~/G/Chapter05 (book_release=)> l
total 132K
drwxrwxr-x 3 dan dan 4.0K Jun  9 06:06 calcpy/
drwxrwxr-x 3 dan dan 4.0K Jun  9 06:06 calcpy_with_cli/
-rw-rw-r-- 1 dan dan  279 Jun  8 21:37 enum43_sample.py
-rw-rw-r-- 1 dan dan  329 Jun  8 21:33 numpy_sample.py
-rw-rw-r-- 1 dan dan  269 Jun  8 21:45 pydub_sample.py
-rw-rw-r-- 1 dan dan   79K Jun  9 23:11 test_audio.mp3
dan@dannixon-envy-ubuntu ~/G/Chapter05 (book_release=)> 
```

Installing modules using pip

One easier alternative to installing packages manually is installing them from the PyPI repository (`pypi.python.org`) using the pip package manager, which is already installed on Raspbian.

To demonstrate this, we will install the `enum34` package (`https://pypi.python.org/pypi/enum34`), which is a version of the enumeration types available in Python 3.4 for lesser Python versions.

Installing a package using `pip` is done using a single command, as follows:

```
sudo pip install enum34
```

This command gives a much more concise output when used to install the packages, as shown in the following screenshot:

```
dan@dannixon-envy-ubuntu -> sudo pip install enum34
Downloading/unpacking enum34
  Downloading enum34-1.0.4.tar.gz
  Running setup.py (path:/tmp/pip_build_root/enum34/setup.py) egg_info for package enum34

Installing collected packages: enum34
  Running setup.py install for enum34

Successfully installed enum34
Cleaning up...
dan@dannixon-envy-ubuntu -> []
```

Once the package is installed, we can demonstrate its usage in a sample script, as follows:

```python
from enum import Enum

class OperatingSystem(Enum):
    Windows = 1
    OSX = 2
    Linux = 3

print OperatingSystem
print dir(OperatingSystem)
print OperatingSystem.Linux
print OperatingSystem.Linux.value
```

This preceding script will output several pieces of information about the enumeration type we just created, as shown in the following screenshot:

```
dan@dannixon-envy-ubuntu ~/G/Chapter05 (book_release=)> python enum43_sample.py
<enum 'OperatingSystem'>
['Linux', 'OSX', 'Windows', '__class__', '__doc__', '__members__', '__module__']
OperatingSystem.Linux
3
dan@dannixon-envy-ubuntu ~/G/Chapter05 (book_release=)> []
```

Installing modules using apt

A further alternative to the pip package manager is using the operating system's default package manager; in the case of Raspbian, it is apt.

Typically, you will not find as many packages on these such repositories as publishing onto them requires developers to maintain their packages on multiple repositories; if they publish to PyPI, however, they only have to maintain a single copy of their package.

```
sudo apt-get install python-numpy
```

This gives the same output as would typically be expected for any package installed with the systems default package manager, as shown in the following screenshot:

```
dan@dannixon-envy-ubuntu -> sudo apt-get install python-numpy
Reading package lists... Done
Building dependency tree
Reading state information... Done
The following packages were automatically installed and are no longer required:
  ipython ipython-qtconsole libgoogle-perftools4 libhdf4-0 libjsoncpp0
  libmxml1 libnexus0 liboce-foundation8 liboce-modeling8 libpgm-5.1-0
  libpococrypto11 libpocofoundation11 libpoconet11 libpoconetssl11
  libpocoutil11 libpocoxml11 libqscintilla2-11 libqscintilla2-l10n libqwt5-qt4
  libqwtplot3d-qt4-0 libtcmalloc-minimal4 libunwind8 libzmq3
  linux-headers-3.13.0-45 linux-headers-3.13.0-45-generic
  linux-image-3.13.0-45-generic linux-image-extra-3.13.0-45-generic
  mypaint-data python-dateutil python-decorator python-matplotlib-data
  python-pyparsing python-simplegeneric python-support python-tz python-zmq
Use 'apt-get autoremove' to remove them.
Suggested packages:
  gfortran python-nose python-numpy-dbg python-numpy-doc
The following NEW packages will be installed
  python-numpy
0 to upgrade, 1 to newly install, 0 to remove and 157 not to upgrade.
Need to get 1,603 kB of archives.
After this operation, 8,758 kB of additional disk space will be used.
Get:1 http://gb.archive.ubuntu.com/ubuntu/ trusty-updates/main python-numpy amd64 1:1.8.2-0ubuntu0.1 [1,603 kB]
Fetched 1,603 kB in 0s (5,436 kB/s)
Selecting previously unselected package python-numpy.
(Reading database ... 454453 files and directories currently installed.)
Preparing to unpack .../python-numpy_1%3a1.8.2-0ubuntu0.1_amd64.deb ...
Unpacking python-numpy (1:1.8.2-0ubuntu0.1) ...
Processing triggers for man-db (2.6.7.1-1ubuntu1) ...
Setting up python-numpy (1:1.8.2-0ubuntu0.1) ...
dan@dannixon-envy-ubuntu -> []
```

We can now import the Numpy library and make use of it in a simple demonstration script, as shown next:

```
import numpy

angles_deg = numpy.array(range(0, 360, 15))
angles_rad = numpy.radians(angles_deg)
angles_sine = numpy.sin(angles_rad)

print "DEG\tRAD\t\tSINE"
for deg, rad, sine in zip(angles_deg, angles_rad, angles_sine):
    print "%d\t%f\t%f" % (deg, rad, sine)
```

This preceding script gives a tabulated set of values, as shown in the following screenshot:

```
dan@dannixon-envy-ubuntu ~/G/Chapter05 (book_release=)> python numpy_sample.py
DEG      RAD             SINE
0        0.000000        0.000000
15       0.261799        0.258819
30       0.523599        0.500000
45       0.785398        0.707107
60       1.047198        0.866025
75       1.308997        0.965926
90       1.570796        1.000000
105      1.832596        0.965926
120      2.094395        0.866025
135      2.356194        0.707107
150      2.617994        0.500000
165      2.879793        0.258819
180      3.141593        0.000000
195      3.403392        -0.258819
210      3.665191        -0.500000
225      3.926991        -0.707107
240      4.188790        -0.866025
255      4.450590        -0.965926
270      4.712389        -1.000000
285      4.974188        -0.965926
300      5.235988        -0.866025
315      5.497787        -0.707107
330      5.759587        -0.500000
345      6.021386        -0.258819
dan@dannixon-envy-ubuntu ~/G/Chapter05 (book_release=)>
```

Packaging your own Python modules

Now that we have seen how the Python packages can be downloaded and installed, we will look at how they can be created from our own modules. For now, we will only look at how they are packaged and leave out the process of publishing it to a repository.

Packaging a library

We will first look at how to package a library that can be imported by other Python scripts and applications.

We will start with a copy of the calculator module that we created in *Chapter 3, Working with Data Structures and I/O*.

1. First, create a new directory named calcpy and move the calculator directory inside it. This calcpy directory will be the packaged library.

2. Now, create an empty Python file named __init__.py inside the calcpy directory using the following command. This file will tell Python that the calcpy directory should be treated as a module.

    touch __init__.py

3. Next, create another directory called calcpy that contains the calcpy directory created in the previous step. This directory will be the package itself.

4. Now, create an empty setup.py file within the calcpy directory created in the previous step. This file will later contain the instructions on how the library will be installed.

By this point, the directory structure should be the same as what is shown in the following tree:

```
dan@dannixon-envy-ubuntu ~/G/C/calcpy (book_release=)> tree .
.
├── calcpy
│   ├── calculator
│   │   ├── Calculator.py
│   │   ├── __init__.py
│   │   └── Operation.py
│   └── __init__.py
└── setup.py

2 directories, 5 files
dan@dannixon-envy-ubuntu ~/G/C/calcpy (book_release=)>
```

Next, open the `setup.py` file and add the following code:

```
from setuptools import setup

setup(
    name="calcpy",
    version="0.0.1",
    description="A basic calculator",
    classifiers=[
        "Natural Language :: English",
        "Programming Language :: Python :: 2.7",
    ],
    author="Dan Nixon",
    packages=["calcpy", "calcpy.calculator"],
    install_requires=[
        "numpy"
    ])
```

In the preceding code, the first line is used to import the `setuptools` utility which will be used to install the module when a user runs the `setup.py` script.

The following lines describe the library or the application that is contained within the module; some are fairly self explanatory (such as `name`, `version`, `description`, and `author`):

- `classifiers`: It is a list of strings that describe the software or the library that is contained within the package. This list is used to help categorize the packages on repositories such as PyPI. A full list of the available classifiers can be found at `https://pypi.python.org/pypi?%3Aaction=list_classifiers`.

- `packages`: It is a list of strings that define the Python modules included in the package. This can be useful to only include the modules that provide functionality and exclude those that only form part of the development process (for example, automated tests).

- `install_requires`: It is a list of strings that define any additional packages that the library requires. These should be the package names as they appear in PyPI. Note that in this example, Numpy is not actually required by this library; it is just included as a demonstration.

Once this is done, you can install the package by running the following command:

```
sudo python setup.py install
```

This should give a message similar to the one shown in the following screenshot:

```
creating build/bdist.linux-x86_64/egg/EGG-INFO
copying calcpy.egg-info/PKG-INFO -> build/bdist.linux-x86_64/egg/EGG-INFO
copying calcpy.egg-info/SOURCES.txt -> build/bdist.linux-x86_64/egg/EGG-INFO
copying calcpy.egg-info/dependency_links.txt -> build/bdist.linux-x86_64/egg/EGG-INFO
copying calcpy.egg-info/requires.txt -> build/bdist.linux-x86_64/egg/EGG-INFO
copying calcpy.egg-info/top_level.txt -> build/bdist.linux-x86_64/egg/EGG-INFO
zip_safe flag not set; analyzing archive contents...
creating dist
creating 'dist/calcpy-0.0.1-py2.7.egg' and adding 'build/bdist.linux-x86_64/egg' to it
removing 'build/bdist.linux-x86_64/egg' (and everything under it)
Processing calcpy-0.0.1-py2.7.egg
removing '/usr/local/lib/python2.7/dist-packages/calcpy-0.0.1-py2.7.egg' (and everything under it)
Copying calcpy-0.0.1-py2.7.egg to /usr/local/lib/python2.7/dist-packages
Removing calcpy 0.0.2 from easy-install.pth file
Adding calcpy 0.0.1 to easy-install.pth file

Installed /usr/local/lib/python2.7/dist-packages/calcpy-0.0.1-py2.7.egg
Processing dependencies for calcpy==0.0.1
Finished processing dependencies for calcpy==0.0.1
dan@dannixon-envy-ubuntu ~/G/C/calcpy (book_release=)>
```

Now, in a new Python shell, you can import the `Calculator` class using the following code:

```
from calcpy.calculator.calculator import Calculator
```

Adding an entry point

We can also use `setuptools` to package full application, both command line and GUI based. We will now have a look at how to modify our existing `calcpy` package to include a command line interface that would be installed alongside the package.

First, we need to create a script that will provide the command line interface. In this case, we will place this script in the `calcpy/calcpy` directory and save it as `cli.py`. The contents of this script are as follows:

```python
from calcpy.calculator.Calculator import Calculator
import sys

def run_cli():
    calc = Calculator()

    for arg in sys.argv[1:]:
        try:
            value = float(arg)
            calc.enter_value(value)
        except ValueError:
            calc.enter_operation(arg)
```

```
        result = calc.evaluate()
        print result


    if __name__ == "__main__":
        run_cli()
```

This is a very simple command line interface that takes the values given to the script from the command line, attempts to build a calculation with them, and then returns the evaluated result.

Next, we need to add the entry point in the `setup.py` script so that the script is automatically added to the users PATH variable when the package is installed, which is required for the script to be used from the command line.

This takes the form of the following addition to the call to the `setup()` function:

```
entry_points={
    "console_scripts": [
        "calcpy = calcpy.cli:run_cli"
    ]
},
```

This addition tells setuptools that there is a console entry point which should be aliased as `calcpy` from the command line and will call the `run_cli` function in the `calcpy/cli.py` Python file.

By now, the `setup.py` script should look something like the following screenshot:

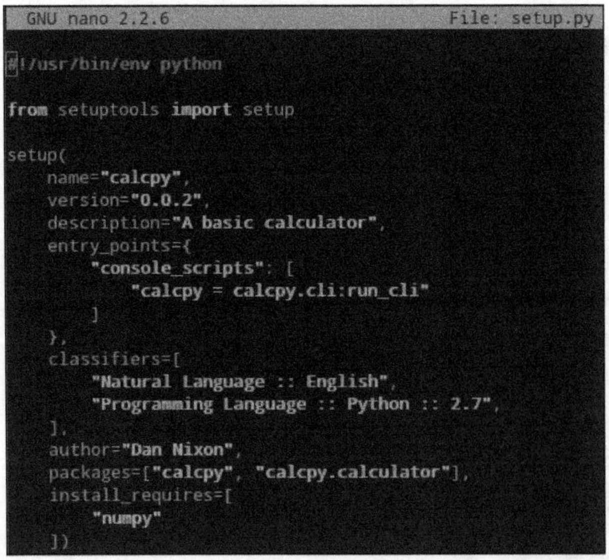

The directory structure should also be similar to what it was before but with the addition of the `cli.py` script, as shown in the following screenshot:

```
dan@dannixon-envy-ubuntu ~/G/C/calcpy_with_cli (book_release=)> tree .
.
├── calcpy
│   ├── calculator
│   │   ├── Calculator.py
│   │   ├── __init__.py
│   │   └── Operation.py
│   ├── cli.py
│   └── __init__.py
└── setup.py

2 directories, 6 files
dan@dannixon-envy-ubuntu ~/G/C/calcpy_with_cli (book_release=)> []
```

Now we can rerun the following installation command to install the new version of the `calcpy` package:

```
sudo python setup.py install
```

This will enable us to use the command line interface to `calcpy` from the terminal by calling the `calcpy` command with several operations and values, as shown in the following screenshot:

```
dan@dannixon-envy-ubuntu ~> calcpy 1 add 3
4.0
dan@dannixon-envy-ubuntu ~> calcpy 1 add 3 subtract 7
-3.0
dan@dannixon-envy-ubuntu ~> []
```

Summary

In this chapter, we first learnt about the most common ways to install third party libraries and how to then use them in our own Python code. Doing this greatly broadens the range of functionality that becomes available to your Python applications.

We then looked at ways that we can package our own Python libraries and application, using the setup tools module ready for distribution to other devices.

In the next chapter, we will start to focus on some of the Raspberry Pi specific side of Python as we start to use the `gpio` library to access and control the GPIO header on the Raspberry Pi.

6
Accessing the GPIO Pins

In this chapter, we will look at the simplest way of interfacing with digital electronics using the **General Purpose Input and Output (GPIO)** port on the Raspberry Pi. To do this, we will be using the `RPi.GPIO` module, which is installed as standard on the newer versions of Raspbian.

We will also take a quick look at some of the basics of digital electronics and the additional methods of communication offered by the Raspberry Pi, including UART.

Note that some of the examples later in the chapter will require some additional electronic components, all of which can be purchased from standard high street electronics retailers.

The components required are:

- A small breadboard
- Some 0.1" male to female jumper wires
- A push to make a switch
- Some LEDs
- The appropriate resistor for the LEDs

The exact value of the resistor can be calculated using an online tool, such as the one found at `ledcalc.com`. Here, the supply voltage should be 3.3V, the LED current should be 20mA, and the number of LEDs should be 1. The voltage drop will depend on the type of LEDs you use (the site has a reasonable guide based on the color of the LED).

Digital electronics

Before we start interfacing the Pi to any electronics, we will first take a look at some of the fundamentals of digital electronics.

Logic in digital electronics is composed of two states: high and low. Typically, low is represented by the signal being close to the ground (0V) and high is represented by being close to a reference voltage (usually, the operating voltage of the logic device). In the case of the Raspberry Pi, it is 3.3V.

 Be sure that any device that you connect to the Raspberry Pi via the GPIO port can operate at 3.3V.

The point at which a signal changes between these two states is known as an **edge**. This can either be rising or falling depending on the direction of the state change, as shown in the following diagram:

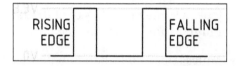

Another concept we will see later in this chapter is **Pulse Width Modulation (PWM)**. This is the concept of simulating an analog signal (a constant signal at a voltage between the high and the low levels) by creating a digital signal and varying the ratio between the time the signal is high and the time it is low (known as the **duty cycle**).

This is demonstrated in the following diagram, where you can see the effects changing the duty cycles has on a signal, which can then be used to control certain devices that can also operate on an analog signal. For example, a common use for PWM is to control the brightness of an LED or other lighting device.

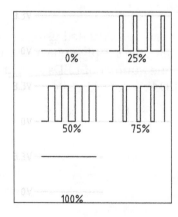

Another concept we will touch on later in the chapter is the idea of pull up and pull down resistors. These are typically high value resistors (10K Ohm is a common value) used on input pins, that would otherwise be left floating (that is, in a state that is neither high or low), to define the normal (or inactive) state of the input.

The GPIO library

The RPi.GPIO module provides a simple interface to the basic digital logic functionality of the GPIO header as well as software synthesized PWM, which allows the Pi to output an analog like signal.

Before starting to use the GPIO pins, it is important to know what each pin can do and what it is connected to. The following diagram shows the pinouts for each version and revision of the Raspberry Pi:

 Note that the Raspberry Pi 2 has the same pinout as the Raspberry Pi B+.

Raspberry Pi B Rev 1				Raspberry Pi A/B Rev 2				Raspberry Pi B+			
3.3V	1	2	5V	3.3V	1	2	5V	3.3V	1	2	5V
GPIO 0	3	4	5V	GPIO 2	3	4	5V	GPIO 2	3	4	5V
GPIO 1	5	6	GND	GPIO 3	5	6	GND	GPIO 3	5	6	GND
GPIO 4	7	8	GPIO 14	GPIO 4	7	8	GPIO 14	GPIO 4	7	8	GPIO 14
GND	9	10	GPIO 15	GND	9	10	GPIO 15	GND	9	10	GPIO 15
GPIO 17	11	12	GPIO 18	GPIO 17	11	12	GPIO 18	GPIO 17	11	12	GPIO 18
GPIO 21	13	14	GND	GPIO 21	13	14	GND	GPIO 21	13	14	GND
GPIO 22	15	16	GPIO 23	GPIO 22	15	16	GPIO 23	GPIO 22	15	16	GPIO 23
3.3V	17	18	GPIO 24	3.3V	17	18	GPIO 24	3.3V	17	18	GPIO 24
GPIO 10	19	20	GND	GPIO 10	19	20	GND	GPIO 10	19	20	GND
GPIO 9	21	22	GPIO 25	GPIO 9	21	22	GPIO 25	GPIO 9	21	22	GPIO 25
GPIO 11	23	24	GPIO 8	GPIO 11	23	24	GPIO 8	GPIO 11	23	24	GPIO 8
GND	25	26	GPIO 7	GND	25	26	GPIO 7	GND	25	26	GPIO 7
								DNC	27	28	DNC
								GPIO 5	29	30	GND
								GPIO 6	31	32	GPIO 12
								GPIO 13	33	34	GND
								GPIO 19	35	36	GPIO 16
								GPIO 26	37	38	GPIO 20
								GND	39	40	GPIO 21

Typically, when using the GPIO pins, you should avoid using the GPIOs 14 and 15 as they are by default used for a serial terminal which provides access to the shell running on the Pi. GPIOs 0, 1, 2, and 3 should also be avoided as they are used for the I2C interface, which requires a pull-up resistor to be used on the pins that is fitted by default and can cause issues with some devices.

Single LED output

To demonstrate the basic use of the GPIO library, we will create a simple script that will flash an LED once a second for 10 seconds. This will require us to build a simple circuit to connect to the GPIO header, as shown in the following diagram:

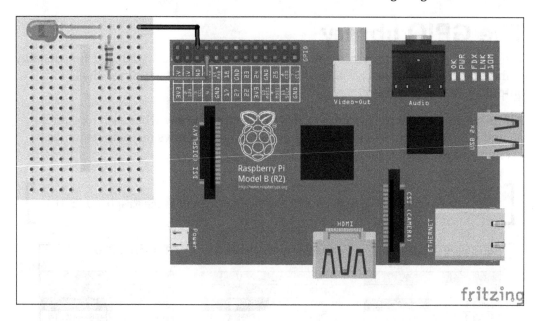

Note that the polarity of the LED is important as electrical current can only flow through it in one direction. The longer lead of the LED is the anode, which should be connected to the resistor, and the shorter lead is the cathode, which should be connected to the ground pin of the Raspberry Pi.

Next, we will start writing the script to blink the LED. This is to be saved as a file named `basic_output.py`. First, we will import the `RPi.GPIO` module and the `sleep` function which will be used later in the code.

```
import RPi.GPIO as GPIO
from time import sleep
```

Next, we will set the numbering mode to use the GPIO numbers rather than the numbers of the pins on the GPIO header.

```
GPIO.setmode(GPIO.BCM)
```

The `led_gpio` variable will hold the GPIO number that the LED will be attached to.

```
led_gpio = 4
```

Next, we will configure the GPIO pin that the LED is connected to as an output.

```
GPIO.setup(led_gpio, GPIO.OUT)
```

Now, we will loop 10 times in order to flash the LED. Note that the iterator variable is not required here, so is replaced with _.

```
for _ in range(10):
```

Here, we are reading the current state of the GPIO pin and then setting it to the negated value. This effectively toggles the state of the pin.

```
GPIO.output(led_gpio, not GPIO.input(led_gpio))
sleep(1.0)
```

Before exiting, the `cleanup` function should be called to reset the configuration and the states of all the GPIO pins. It is possible to clean up the individual pins, however, it is only an issue when running multiple applications that access the GPIO pins simultaneously.

```
GPIO.cleanup()
```

Once the code has been written, the script can be executed using the following command:

```
sudo python basic_output.py
```

The script will not produce any output on the terminal, however, you will see the LED flash on and off once per second. If not, then ensure that the wiring is correct and that the LED is inserted in the correct polarity.

 Scripts that use the `gpio` module must be executed using `sudo` as access to the GPIO port requires root privileges.

PWM output

We can also control the brightness of the LED using PWM with no changes to the circuit used previously. This allows us to set the LED brightness to any level between off and fully on.

It is worth noting that the brightness of the LED does not change linearly with the duty cycle used to dim it. However, for the examples used next, this will not be an issue.

We start the Python file in the same way as the previous example. This time we will save the file as pwm_output.py.

```
import RPi.GPIO as GPIO
from time import sleep
```

Next, we will define a function that will fade a PWM output from a given duty cycle to another, with a given number of steps between the values.

```
def do_fade(pwm, start, end, step=2):
    if start > end:
        step *= -1
        end -= 1
    else:
        end += 1
    for duty in range(start, end, step):
        pwm.ChangeDutyCycle(duty)
        sleep(0.1)
```

Now, we will configure the GPIO numbering and the output pin in the same way as was done in the previous example.

```
GPIO.setmode(GPIO.BCM)
led_gpio = 4
GPIO.setup(led_gpio, GPIO.OUT)
```

Next, we will create a PWM object which manages the output of the PWM signal. Here, we are creating the PWM object on the led_gpio pin at an output frequency of 50Hz. The second line starts the PWM signal and sets the initial duty cycle.

```
pwm = GPIO.PWM(led_gpio, 50)
pwm.start(0)
```

Now, we will fade the LED on and off twice.

```
for _ in range(2):
    do_fade(pwm, 0, 100)
    do_fade(pwm, 100, 0)
```

Finally, clean up the GPIO configuration.

```
GPIO.cleanup()
```

As with the previous script, this can be executed with the following command:

```
sudo python pwm_output.py
```

This script does not produce any output on the terminal but you should see the LED slowly fade from off to fully on twice.

Multiple outputs

The GPIO library also provides some nice functionality for modifying multiple GPIO pins simultaneously. This can help keep the code clean when working with multiple devices or devices that require multiple GPIO pins.

To demonstrate this, we will add an additional LED to the current circuit, as shown in the following diagram:

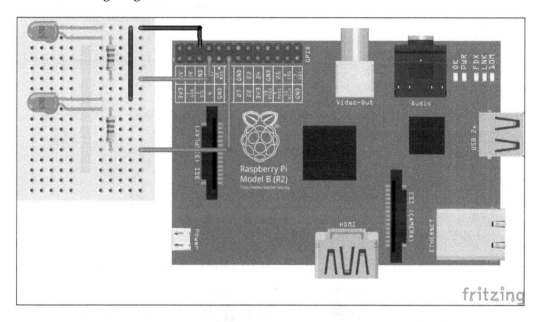

We start the Python file in the usual way. This time we will save the file as `multiple_output.py`.

```
import RPi.GPIO as GPIO
from time import sleep
GPIO.setmode(GPIO.BCM)
```

Next, we will define a list of the GPIO pins that will be used as outputs for LEDs and set each of them up as an output. Here, we are also setting the initial state of each output, where every other LED is set low.

```
led_gpios = [4, 17]
for i, gpio in enumerate(led_gpios):
    state = i % 2 == 0
    GPIO.setup(gpio, GPIO.OUT, initial=state)
```

Next, we will loop 10 times and toggle the state of each GPIO pin. Here, we are passing `list` for both the GPIO number and the output states in the call to `GPIO.output`.

```
for _ in range(10):
    states = [not GPIO.input(gpio) for gpio in led_gpios]
    GPIO.output(led_gpios, states)
    sleep(1.0)
```

Finally, we will reset the GPIO configuration before the script exits.

```
GPIO.cleanup()
```

Once the file is saved, it can be executed as earlier, using the following command:

sudo python multiple_output.py

This script will also output nothing to the terminal but you will see the two LEDs flash with opposite states 10 times before they both turn off.

Basic switch

Now that we have seen how the GPIO library can be used to control the output devices, we will have a look at how it can be used to read the state of the GPIO pins to determine the state of the input devices, such as buttons and switches.

To start us off, we will look at a simple switch, as shown in the following diagram:

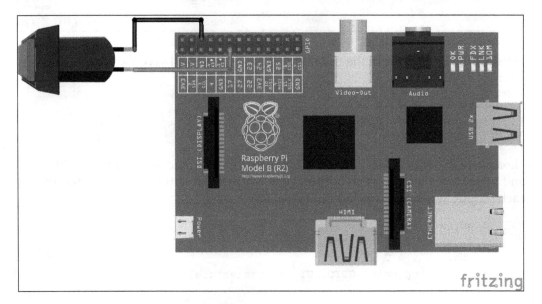

No additional circuitry is required here as the Raspberry Pi's GPIO pins can be configured to connect an internal pull up or pull down resistor to each GPIO pin, as we will see later in the example.

We start the Python file in the usual way. This time we will save the file as `basic_input.py`.

```
import RPi.GPIO as GPIO
from time import sleep
GPIO.setmode(GPIO.BCM)
```

Now, we will define the GPIO pin the switch is connected to and configure it as an input.

```
switch_gpio = 17
GPIO.setup(switch_gpio, GPIO.IN, pull_up_down=GPIO.PUD_UP)
```

Now, we will loop forever, reading the state of the switch every second and printing the state to the terminal.

```
try:
    while(True):
        state = not GPIO.input(switch_gpio)
        print "Switch is pressed: %d" % state
        sleep(1.0)
```

Finally, we will catch the `KeyboardInterrupt` exception, which is raised when the user presses *Ctrl - C* to exit a program, and use this as a signal to reset the GPIO configuration and exit.

```
except KeyboardInterrupt:
    GPIO.cleanup()
```

Once the script is saved, it can be executed using the following command:

```
sudo python basic_input.py
```

Once running, the script will start outputting the state of the switch pin, as shown in the following screenshot:

```
pi@raspberrypi ~ $ sudo python basic_input.py
Switch is pressed: 0
Switch is pressed: 0
Switch is pressed: 0
Switch is pressed: 0
Switch is pressed: 1
Switch is pressed: 1
Switch is pressed: 0
Switch is pressed: 1
Switch is pressed: 1
Switch is pressed: 1
```

Switch using interrupt

Another option for reading input from devices is to configure an interrupt that will watch the state of the GPIO pin and call a function in a separate thread when the state changed is a certain way.

To demonstrate this, we will use both a switch and a LED in a circuit, as shown in the following diagram:

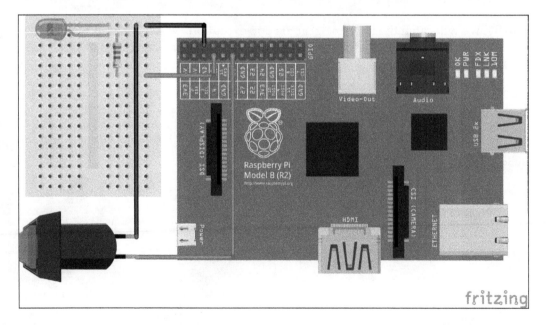

We will start the Python script in the usual way. This time we will save the file as `interrupt_input.py`.

```
import RPi.GPIO as GPIO
from time import sleep
GPIO.setmode(GPIO.BCM)
```

Next, we will define the GPIO pins that the LED and the switch are connected to.

```
led_gpio = 4
switch_gpio = 17
```

Now, setup the GPIO pins for their functions.

```
GPIO.setup(led_gpio, GPIO.OUT)
GPIO.setup(switch_gpio, GPIO.IN, pull_up_down=GPIO.PUD_UP)
```

Define the function to be called when the switch button is pressed. This is denoted by the falling edge, as the pin will be going from high when the switch is open and to low when the switch connects the pin to the ground.

Also, note that the callback functions can take a parameter; it is the GPIO number that the interrupt was triggered by. In this case, we are ignoring it as we have no use for it.

```
def toggle_led(_):
    GPIO.output(led_gpio, not GPIO.input(led_gpio))
```

Attach the created callback function to the GPIO library. Here, we are only using the interrupt for the falling edges. It is also possible to detect the rising and both the edges using RISING and BOTH in place of FALLING in the following line:

```
GPIO.add_event_detect(switch_gpio, GPIO.FALLING,
callback=toggle_led, bouncetime=500)
```

Here, the `bouncetime` parameter is used to limit the minimum time between the interrupts being fired by the button changing state. This is a technique known as **debounceing**.

We will have the main thread do very little work since the callback is handled in a separate thread. As earlier, this allows you to exit the program using *Ctrl - C*.

```
try:
    while(True):
        sleep(1.0)
except KeyboardInterrupt:
    GPIO.cleanup()
```

Once the script is complete, it can be executed with the following command:

```
sudo python interrupt_input.py
```

This script does not create any output on the terminal. However, when the switch is pressed, you will see the state of the LED get toggled; specifically, the LED should change state when the switch is pressed and do nothing when the switch is released. However, it is normal to occasionally see the LED change state twice, particularly if the switch contacts made a poor connection.

Universal Asynchronous Receiver/ Transmitter (UART)

The Raspberry Pi also has a **Universal Asynchronous Receiver/Transmitter (UART)** connection on the GPIO header that can be used to interface with external hardware (such as an Arduino). Fortunately, it is easy to use through the pySerial Python library (`https://pypi.python.org/pypi/pyserial`), which provides access to the serial ports on a variety of platforms.

Setting up the serial port

Before we can use the serial port on the Raspberry Pi, there are a couple of configuration files that must first be changed to stop Raspbian from using the port as an additional terminal, which would otherwise cause communication issues if another piece of software attempted to use the port.

The first file that requires modification is `/boot/cmdline.txt`. Open this file as root using the following command in the terminal:

```
sudo nano /boot/cmdline.txt
```

Here, we need to remove `console=ttyAMA0,115200` from the single line of the file; doing so tells the Pi not to use the serial port when it is booting.

Once completed, the file should look similar to what is shown in the following screenshot:

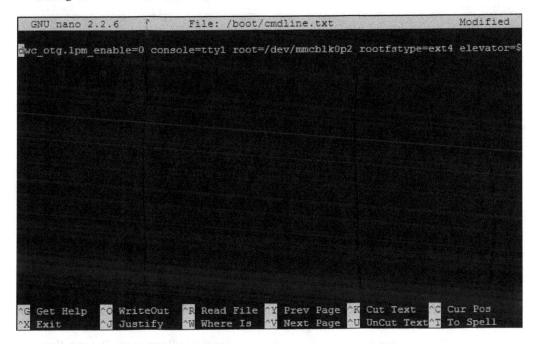

Once done, press *Ctrl - X* followed by *Y* to exit nano and return to the terminal.

The next file is /etc/inittab which must also be modified as the root user.

```
sudo nano /etc/inittab
```

Here, we need to search for and comment out the following line. This will disable the terminal being launched on the serial port once Raspbian boots.

```
2:23:respawn:/sbin/getty -L ttyAMA0 115200 vt100
```

Once done, the file should look similar to the one shown in the following screenshot:

```
  GNU nano 2.2.6                  File: /etc/inittab                    Modified

6:23:respawn:/sbin/getty 38400 tty6

# Example how to put a getty on a serial line (for a terminal)
#
#T0:23:respawn:/sbin/getty -L ttyS0 9600 vt100
#T1:23:respawn:/sbin/getty -L ttyS1 9600 vt100

# Example how to put a getty on a modem line.
#
#T3:23:respawn:/sbin/mgetty -x0 -s 57600 ttyS3


#Spawn a getty on Raspberry Pi serial line
#T0:23:respawn:/sbin/getty -L ttyAMA0 115200 vt100




^G Get Help    ^O WriteOut    ^R Read File   ^Y Prev Page   ^K Cut Text    ^C Cur Pos
^X Exit        ^J Justify     ^W Where Is    ^V Next Page   ^U UnCut Text  ^T To Spell
```

Finally, save the changes to /etc/inittab and reboot the Raspberry Pi with the following command:

```
sudo reboot
```

Using pySerial

Once the required modifications to the terminal configuration are done, the pySerial library can be installed through the pip package manager, using the following command:

```
sudo pip install --upgrade pyserial
```

The --upgrade flag is used to update the existing installation, should it already be included with the operating system, or other software or libraries.

As an example, we will simply connect the transmit and receive pins of the Raspberry Pis UART connection on the GPIO header together; this way, any data that the Raspberry Pi transmits it immediately receives.

This can be done by connecting pins 8 and 10 together, as shown in the following diagram:

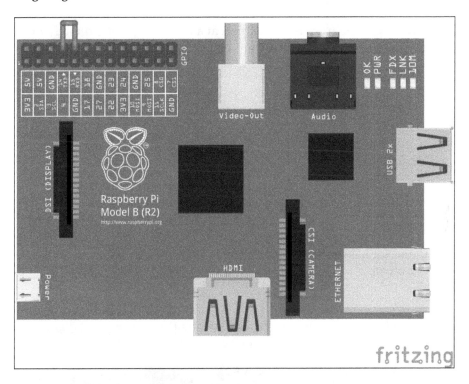

Now, we will use the pySerial library to write a sample script that will send some data to the serial port and read it back. We will save this file as `pyserial_loopback.py`.

First, we need to import the libraries that we will use.

```
import sys
import serial
```

Now, we will create and open the serial port object. Here, we are providing the path to the serial port device (in this case, for the on board serial port), the baud rate (the rate of data transfer in bits per second), and the read timeout is seconds.

```
port = serial.Serial("/dev/ttyAMA0", baudrate=9600, timeout=1)
```

 Note that the baud rate has several standard values that must be used for communication. These include: 110, 300, 600, 1200, 2400, 4800, 9600, 14400, 19200, 38400, 57600, 115200, 128000,, and 256000.

Now that the port is created, we can send some data as a Python string.

```
port.write('Hello, world!')
```

Next, we will read a byte from the serial port at a time and print it directly to the terminal until the `read` function times out, indicating that we have reached the end of the message.

```
while True:
    c = port.read()
    if len(c) == 0:
        break
    sys.stdout.write(c)
sys.stdout.write('\n')
```

Once finished, we will close the serial port before the script exits.

```
port.close()
```

Now that the script has been written, we can save it and execute it using the following command:

```
sudo python pyserial_loopback.py
```

This should produce the following output, showing that the serial port is functioning correctly:

```
pi@raspberrypi ~ $ sudo python pyserial_loopback.py
Hello, world!
pi@raspberrypi ~ $
```

You can also try removing the wire link and running the script again, which will result in the script exiting without printing any output to the terminal.

Additional libraries

While the `RPI.GPIO` module will certainly be sufficient for simple digital logic, you may find that you need to interface to a device that requires the use of one of the communication protocols supported by the Raspberry Pi, such as I2C or SPI.

Fortunately, there are Python libraries available that can do this; for I2C there is smbus-cffi (`https://pypi.python.org/pypi/smbus-cffi`) and SPI can be used through py-spidev (`https://github.com/doceme/py-spidev`).

Summary

In this chapter, we looked at the ways in which the Raspberry Pi can interact with external hardware through basic digital logic and how this can be done using the RPI.GPIO Python module.

In the next chapter, we will continue looking at Pi specific hardware when we take a look at the camera module and its accompanying Python library.

7
Using the Camera Module

In this chapter, we will look at the process for setting up the Raspberry Pi camera module and the picamera Python module (`https://github.com/waveform80/picamera`) that can be used to control the camera, take photos, and record video.

Setting up the camera module

First, we must unpack and connect the camera to the Raspberry Pi. When unboxing the camera module, it is important to avoid exposing the camera to any static electricity that may build up on surfaces and clothes; the camera module is quite sensitive to this, and this has been a common cause of failure of the camera module. This can be avoided by touching an exposed earth connection (for example, a water pipe or unpainted metal case of an appliance).

When the camera module is out of the box, you will notice that one side of the disconnected end of the white flat flex cable has a piece of rigid blue plastic on it (the side opposite to the one with the row of 15 silver contacts), as shown in the following photograph. This is the side of the connector that must face the Ethernet port when inserted into the connector on the Raspberry Pi.

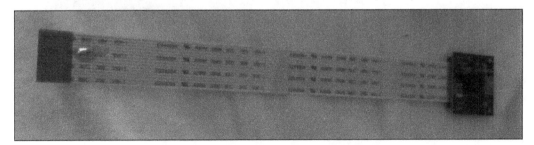

Looking at the Raspberry Pi, you will see two long thin connectors; one near the Ethernet and HDMI ports, and one near the power and GPIO ports (the exact positioning depends on the model of the Raspberry Pi but this is a good guide for all boards). The connecter for the camera is the one near the Ethernet and HDMI ports, as shown in the following image (the Raspberry Pi here is a model B+):

To connect the camera, first lift up the retaining bracket on the connector so that the end of the flat flex connector slots into the connector easily. Once the cable is fully inserted and leveled in the connector, press down on the retaining bracket, and the cable should be held firmly in the connector, as shown in the following image:

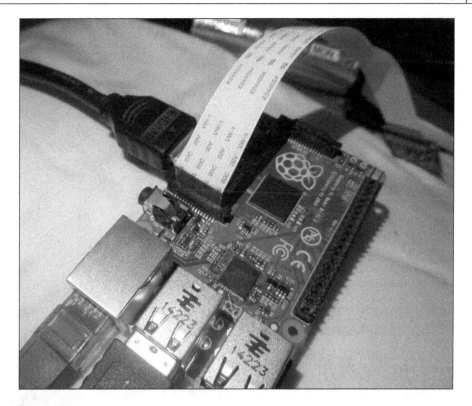

Now that the camera is connected, we will enable it in Raspbian using the
raspi-config utility.

1. Open a terminal and start the utility using the following command:

    sudo raspi-config

2. Using the arrow keys, navigate to the option **5 Enable Camera** and
    select it by pressing *Enter*:

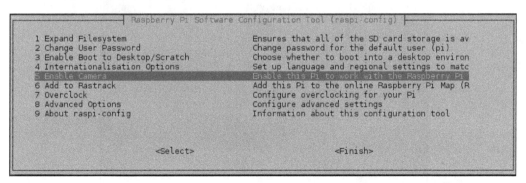

3.   Using the arrow keys, select **Enable** and press *Enter*:

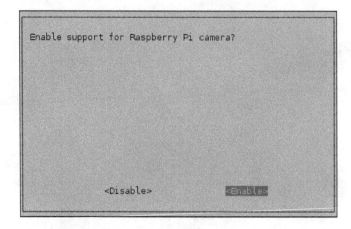

4.   Using the arrow keys, select **Finish** and press *Enter*:

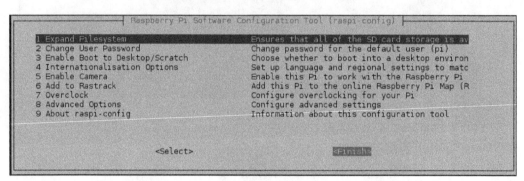

5.   When asked to reboot, press *Enter* to select **Yes**:

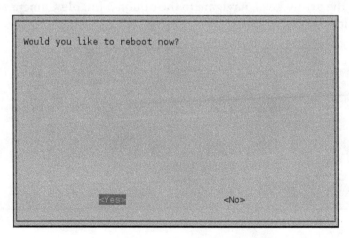

Now that the camera module is enabled and the Pi has rebooted, we can test the camera module using the `raspistill` utility to ensure that it is working correctly.

To do a basic test to see that the camera is working, we can use the following command to open the camera and display a feed on the connected monitor:

```
raspistill -t 0
```

This preceding command should give an output on the display similar to the following image:

Note that this requires you to have a monitor attached via either an HDMI or a composite video, as the output from the camera is rendered directly on the **GPU (Graphical Processing Unit)** rather than in the desktop environment in Raspbian.

We can also use the following command to save a still image as a JPEG file. Here, the `-t` parameter controls the amount of time in milliseconds between the camera preview starting and the image being captured.

```
raspistill -t 5000 -o image.png
```

Note that it is important that the `-t` parameter is greater than around 1000ms to allow the camera time to obtain good auto exposure parameters. If the time is too short then you may end up with images that are either too dark or too light.

There are many other options that can be configured for the camera module, most of which are available in `raspistill`. To see a full list of the options, you can use the following command to get a list of the parameters that can be passed to `raspistill`:

```
raspistill --help 2>&1 | less
```

Installing and testing the Python library

Now that we have the camera module installed and working, we can install and start using the `picamera` library.

1. First, we need to install the pip package manager in order to install the latest version of the `picamera` library. This can be done using the following command:

   ```
   sudo apt-get install python-pip
   ```

2. Next, we will update the installed version of the `picamera` library using the following command:

   ```
   sudo pip install --upgrade picamera
   ```

Now that the library is installed, we can test it out with a basic example to ensure that both the camera and the library are working correctly. This also gives us a chance to look at the basic usage of the `picamera` library.

We will do this from an interactive Python shell. First, we will import the required libraries:

```
import time
from picamera import PiCamera
```

Next, we will use the `with` statement to manage opening and closing the camera:

```
with PiCamera() as cam:
```

Now, we will set the resolution the camera will capture at and start the preview, which allows the camera to start automatic exposure correction:

```
cam.resolution = (1024, 768)
cam.start_preview()
```

Similar to the requirement for the `-t` parameter in `raspistill` to be at least 1 second, we will now wait 2 seconds before capturing any images:

```
time.sleep(2)
```

Finally, we will capture a still image and save it as `python_image.jpg` in the current directory:

```
cam.capture("python_image.jpg")
```

After this, the camera will be closed automatically as control flow will exit the `with` block. You can now open the `python_image.jpg` file that was saved. This minimal working example will be the basis of the rest of the scripts that we will look at in this chapter.

Writing applications for the camera

Now, we will look at a few different possible uses for the camera module and some of the functionality of the `picamera` library. While this covers the basics of using the module, it may also be worth a look at the library documentation at `picamera.readthedocs.org` to learn more about the functionality offered by the library.

A time lapse recorder

The first example we will look at is a simple timelapse still recorder. Essentially, all this will do is capture a series of still images with a given delay between each image.

The code for the Python script that will do this is as follows. First, we will import all the libraries and functions that we will use in the script:

```
import sys
import os
from string import Template
from time import sleep
from threading import Thread
from picamera import PiCamera
```

Next, we will create a `thread` class that will perform the still image capture:

```
class ImageCapture(Thread):
    def __init__(self, filename, resolution=None, delay=1.0):
        Thread.__init__(self)
        self._filename = filename
        self._delay = delay
        self._resolution = resolution if resolution is not None
else (1024, 768)    def run(self):
        with PiCamera() as cam:
            cam.resolution = self._resolution
            cam.start_preview()
            sleep(self._delay)
            cam.capture(self._filename)
```

This is essentially the basic still image capture example that we used in the interactive terminal previously, wrapped in a `Thread` class so that it can be performed asynchronously from the main thread. We use this technique so that the time between the images is not skewed by the time taken for the image capture process, which is not a constant time. Hence, simply adding a delay between the calls to `capture` may not give a reliable delay between the images.

Next, we will do some very basic command line parsing in order to get the delay between the images and the directory in which to save the captured images from the command line input. To do this, we are simply using sys.argv, which gives a list of all input from the command line when a script is executed:

```
delay = float(sys.argv[1])
save_directory = sys.argv[2]
```

Now, we will check to see if the directory in which the images will be saved already exists on the file system; if it does not, then we will create it. This is done using the os module:

```
if not os.path.exists(save_directory):
    os.makedirs(save_directory)
```

Now, we will create a string template that will be used to determine the filename of a captured image:

```
filename_format = Template("${frameno}_img.jpg")
```

Finally, we will set up a loop that will start a new image capture thread with a delay of the number of seconds provided on the command line:

```
frame_no = 0
while True:
    filename = os.path.join(save_directory,
filename_format.substitute(frameno=frame_no))
    ImageCapture(filename).start()
    frame_no += 1
    sleep(delay)
```

Once the script has been completed, save it as timelapse_recorder.py. It can now be executed using the following command:

python timelapse_recorder.py 60 ~/tl_capture

The script does not produce any output to the terminal. However, if you open a file manager, you should start to see images being saved to the directory that you specified (~/tl_capture in this case) at the given timelapse interval (60 seconds in this case).

You will also see the preview image displayed on the entire screen when the image is about to be taken.

Ctrl - C can be used when you wish to end the timelapse capture.

A point-and-shoot camera

This example will use two switches connected to the GPIO port to produce a simple point and shoot camera capable of recording both still images and video.

Firstly, we will connect the two switches to the Raspberry Pi, as shown in the following diagram. One switch should be a push to make switch, and the other a single pole toggle switch. The push to make switch will be used to start and stop the capture, and the toggle switch will switch between the photo and video capture modes.

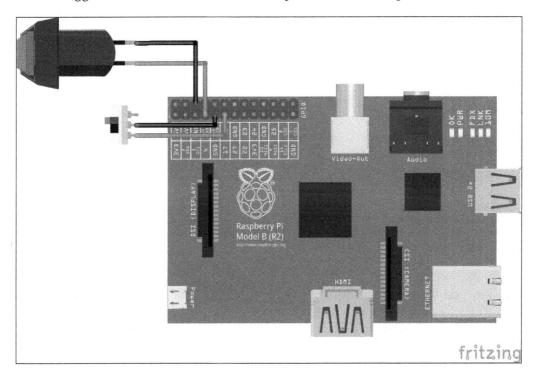

As earlier, we will start the Python script by including the modules and functions used by the script:

```
import sys
import os
from datetime import datetime
from string import Template
from time import sleep, time
from picamera import PiCamera
import RPi.GPIO as GPIO
```

This script will take a single parameter for the directory in which to store the captured photos and videos. This code is the same as was used in the previous example to parse this parameter and create the directory if it did not already exist:

```
save_directory = sys.argv[1]
if not os.path.exists(save_directory):
    os.makedirs(save_directory)
```

Next, we are defining the GPIO pins used for each switch:

```
capture_sw_gpio = 4
capture_mode_gpio = 17
```

This function is used to capture a still image and is called by an event handler on the capture button. This code is very similar to the first example shown in this chapter, except that the delay here is given by the capture button still being held rather than a fixed amount of time.

```
def capture_still(filename, resolution=None):
    print "Still mode"
    with PiCamera() as cam:
        cam.resolution = resolution if resolution is not None else
(1280, 720)
        cam.start_preview()
        while not GPIO.input(capture_sw_gpio):
            sleep(0.5)
        cam.capture(filename)
```

This function is used to capture a video and is called by the event handler for the capture button. Here, you will notice that instead of the `sleep` function, we are using the `wait_recording` function of the camera object. This function performs error checking of the video stream while it is in the delay loop, ensuring that errors are reported immediately rather than on the final call to `stop_recording`.

```
def capture_video(filename, resolution=None):
    print "Video mode"
    with PiCamera() as cam:
        cam.resolution = resolution if resolution is not None else
(640, 480)
        cam.start_recording(filename)
        while not GPIO.input(capture_sw_gpio):
            cam.wait_recording(0.5)
        cam.stop_recording()
```

This function is the event handler for the capture button that is called when the button is pressed. This function is responsible for determining the capture mode based on the status of the capture mode switch, generating a filename for the captured media, and calling the appropriate capture function.

```
def handle_capture_start(_):
    print "Starting capture"
    mode_sw = GPIO.input(capture_mode_gpio)
    mode = 'still' if mode_sw else 'video'
    ext = 'jpg' if mode_sw else 'h264'
    timestamp = datetime.fromtimestamp(time()).
strftime('%Y%m%d_%H%M%S')
    filename =
Template("${datetime}_${mode}.${ext}").substitute(mode=mode,
ext=ext, datetime=timestamp)
    filepath = os.path.join(save_directory, filename)
    if mode == 'still':
        capture_still(filepath)
    elif mode == 'video':
        capture_video(filepath)
    print "Capture saved to: " + filepath
```

Next, we will setup the GPIO pins. Both pins for the switches have the pull up resistors enabled and an event handler is added to the capture button pin that calls the `handle_capture_start` function when the button is pressed.

```
GPIO.setmode(GPIO.BCM)
GPIO.setup(capture_sw_gpio, GPIO.IN, pull_up_down=GPIO.PUD_UP)
GPIO.setup(capture_mode_gpio, GPIO.IN, pull_up_down=GPIO.PUD_UP)
GPIO.add_event_detect(capture_sw_gpio, GPIO.FALLING,
callback=handle_capture_start, bouncetime=500)
```

Here, we will have the main thread do nothing as all the image capture is done in the thread created by the GPIO event handler. We will also add a try-catch block so that the GPIO configuration is cleared when *Ctrl - C* is used to exit the script.

```
try:
    while True:
        sleep(1)
except KeyboardInterrupt:
    GPIO.cleanup()
```

Finally, save the script as `point_shoot_camera.py` and execute it using the following command:

```
sudo python point_shoot_camera.py ~/captures
```

Once the script is running, try pressing the capture button for around 3 seconds. You will start to see output similar to that shown in the following screenshot appear on the terminal.

When in photo mode (the mode switch is open), the preview is started when the capture button is first pressed and continues until it is released once more, at which point the photo is taken.

In video mode (the mode switch is closed), pressing the capture button starts video recording. The recording continues while the capture button is held and stops when it is released.

```
pi@raspberrypi ~ $ sudo python point_shoot_camera.py ~/captures
Starting capture
Video mode
Capture saved to: /home/pi/captures/20150623_212718_video.h264
Starting capture
Video mode
Capture saved to: /home/pi/captures/20150623_212721_video.h264
Starting capture
Still mode
Capture saved to: /home/pi/captures/20150623_212731_still.jpg
Starting capture
Still mode
Capture saved to: /home/pi/captures/20150623_212734_still.jpg
^Cpi@raspberrypi ~ $ 
```

An image effect randomizer

The next script is a simple demonstration script that applies randomized image and color effects to a still image captured from the camera.

We will once again start our Python script by importing the required libraries and functions that we are using in the script:

```
import sys
from random import randint
from time import sleep
from picamera import PiCamera
import RPi.GPIO as GPIO
```

Next, we will get some input from the command line; specifically, the filename to save the captured still image as and the type of effect randomization desired:

```
filename = sys.argv[1]
effect_type = sys.argv[2]
```

Here, we will provide some basic validation for the effect randomization type provided via the command line. This is as simple as checking if the option is one of the three valid options and exiting with a message to the user if not.

```
if effect_type not in ['colour', 'filter', 'both']:
    print "Effect type must be one of: colour, filter, both"
    sys.exit(1)
```

If either the `colour` or `both` option was selected as the effect type, then we will now generate a random color effect. This is done by setting a random integer between 0 and 256 for the U and V modifier values, which are used to scale the U and V color components of the YUV image (`https://en.wikipedia.org/wiki/YUV`):

```
colour = None
if effect_type in ['colour', 'both']:
    colour = (randint(0, 256), randint(0, 256))
    print "Colour effect: " + str(colour)
```

If either the `filter` or `both` option was selected, then we will choose a random image effect to be applied to the image:

```
image_effect = 'none'
if effect_type in ['filter', 'both']:
    image_effect = PiCamera.IMAGE_EFFECTS.keys()[randint(0,
len(PiCamera.IMAGE_EFFECTS))]
    print "Filter: " + image_effect
```

Now, we will start the capture. Note here the additional two lines that set the color and the image effects. We will also use a longer preview time to keep the live preview on the screen for longer.

```
with PiCamera() as cam:
    cam.resolution = (1280, 720)
    cam.image_effect=image_effect
    cam.color_effects=colour
    cam.start_preview()
    sleep(15)
    cam.capture(filename)
```

Finally, save the Python script as `random_effects.py` and execute it using the following command:

python random_effects.py img.jpg both

This will randomize both the color and the image effects. You can also change both to either `colour` or `filter` in order to randomize just one of the effects.

When the script is executed, it will print the values for the effects that were applied to the terminal, as shown in the following screenshot:

```
pi@raspberrypi ~ $ sudo python random_effects.py img.jpg both
Colour effect: (130, 182)
Filter: colorpoint
```

Summary

In this chapter, we looked at the process of setting up the Raspberry Pi camera module and how it can be tested using the raspistill utility bundled by default with Raspbian.

We then went on to use the picamera Python library to control the camera in a variety of situations with customized Python scripts.

In the next chapter, we will look at ways in which a Python application can extract data from online sources.

8

Extracting Data from the Internet

In this chapter, we will look at ways we can extract data and files from the Internet using a range of data formats and services, namely web services (or **Application Protocol Interfaces (APIs)**) using the **Extensible Markup Language (XML)** and **JavaScript Object Notation (JSON)** data formats.

We will also look at how we can use Python to download files and extract information from web pages for when a website does not offer an API to access their data.

Using urllib2 to download data

Before we get on to processing the data we extract from the online sources, we will first demonstrate use of the in-built `urllib2` Python module for downloading data from the internet.

This will be used in all the examples later on in the chapter for parsing information downloaded from the various online sources.

In the following example, we will write a simple script that will download the text contents of a web page and print them to the terminal. This is not a practical use for this module, however it does demonstrate the use of the module for retrieving data from web resources.

We will start by importing the Python modules required for this script. We will save this script file as `urllib_example.py`:

```
import urllib2
import sys
```

In this line, we are taking the first argument on the command line as a URL to open and return the HTML contents of:

```
url = sys.argv[1]
```

Now, we will create a request object that represents a request to be sent to the web server. This is not strictly required in this example, however, we will see its use later on in the chapter.

```
request = urllib2.Request(url)
```

Once the request object has been created and configured, it can be sent to the server using the following line. This will request the data from the server and return a response object.

```
response = urllib2.urlopen(request)
```

In the following lines, we are retrieving the response as a string and displaying it to the terminal:

```
data = response.read()
print data
```

Once the script is completed, it can be executed using the following command. Note that the URL you provide to the script is not critical and can be set to any valid web address.

python urllib_example.py http://google.com

This will produce an output similar to the following screenshot:

Parsing JSON APIs

In this section, we will be creating a simple currency converter application that will be run from the command line using the free to use `Fixer.io` API (`http://fixer.io`) to provide the exchange rates, which are updated daily (which is less frequent than some other paid for APIs, but will be good enough for our use).

This is a JSON API; an example URL is: `http:// api.fixer.io/ latest?base=GBP&symbols=JPY,EUR`

This is making a request for the exchange rates to convert British pounds to Euro and Yen and returns data in the format:

```
{
    "base": "GBP",
    "date": "2015-07-08",
    "rates": {
        "JPY": 186.64,
        "EUR": 1.3941
    }
}
```

As we will see in the next code, this data can be parsed using the `json` Python module, which will return the structure of the JSON tree as a nested tree of Python dictionaries.

We will start by importing the required Python modules for this script, which we will save as `currency_converter.py`:

```
import urllib2
import json
from string import Template
import sys
```

Now, we will define a string template, which will be used to create URLs for the given API calls. Here, the string has two substitutions: one for the currency symbol to be converted from, and another for a comma separated list of the currency symbols to convert to.

```
URL_TEMLATE =
Template('http://api.fixer.io/latest?base=${from_curr}&symbols=$
{to_curr}')
```

The `get_rates` function is used to retrieve a set of exchange rates for a given base currency and a list of target currencies:

```
def get_rates(from_curr, to_currs):
    target_currencies = ','.join(to_currs)
```

```
    api_url = URL_TEMLATE.substitute(from_curr=from_curr,
                                      to_curr=target_currencies)
    response = urllib2.urlopen(api_url)
    json_response = response.read()
```

The following two lines are the lines that parse the JSON data and select the section containing the exchange rates, which is returned as a Python dictionary:

```
    result = json.loads(json_response)
    return result['rates']
```

The `convert` function is responsible for taking a dictionary of the exchange rates and converting a value in the original currency to a value in each of the target currencies. The results of the conversion are returned as a list of dictionaries for each target currency.

```
def convert(from_value, from_curr, to_currs):
    rates = get_rates(from_curr, to_currs)
    conversions = list()
    for symbol in to_currs:
        new_value = rates[symbol] * from_value
        conversion = {'symbol':symbol,
                      'rate': rates[symbol],
                      'value': new_value}
        conversions.append(conversion)
    return conversions
```

The `process_cli` function is used to read the original currency and value, as well as the list of target currencies to convert from the command line arguments and calls to the other functions; the conversion then prints the results on the terminal.

```
def process_cli(params):
    value_to_convert = float(params[0])
    start_currency = params[1].upper()
    conversion_currencies = [curr.upper() for curr in params[3:]]
    conversions = convert(value_to_convert,
                          start_currency,
                          conversion_currencies)
    print '%.2f %s in:' % (value_to_convert, start_currency)
    print 'CURRENCY\tRATE\t\tVALUE'
    for c in conversions:
        print '%s\t\t%.2f\t\t%.2f' % (c['symbol'], c['rate'],
c['value'])
```

This next final piece of code calls the `process_cli` function when the script is run as a standalone script:

```
if __name__ == "__main__":
    process_cli(sys.argv[1:])
```

Once the file has been saved, it can be executed using commands in the same format, as shown next:

python currency_converter.py 345.453 GBP in usd jpy cad Eur

Note that the case of the currency symbols is not important. This will create an output similar to that shown in the following screenshot:

Parsing XML APIs

In this section, we will look at creating a simple weather forecast application using the OpenWeatherMap 5 day forecast API (http://openweathermap.org/forecast#5days), which can return an XML document containing the forecast data.

This API is accessed through a URL in the following format; in this case, we are searching for the weather in Harwell, UK:

```
http://api.openweathermap.org/data/2.5/forecast?q=Harwell,
GB&mode=xml
```

This gives an output in the following format, where the `time` element is repeated for the number of forecasts that are available in the 5 day time range:

```
<?xml version="1.0" encoding="UTF-8"?>
<weatherdata>
    <location>
        <name>Harwell</name>
        <type />
        <country>GB</country>
        <timezone />
        <location altitude="0" latitude="51.599468" longitude="
-1.29175" geobase="geonames" geobaseid="0" />
    </location>
    <credit />
```

```
<meta>
    <lastupdate />
    <calctime>0.0443</calctime>
    <nextupdate />
</meta>
<sun rise="2015-07-08T03:57:59" set="2015-07-08T20:22:06" />
<forecast>
    <time from="2015-07-08T18:00:00" to="2015-07-08T21:00:00">
        <symbol number="800" name="sky is clear" var="01n" />
        <precipitation />
        <windDirection deg="317.004" code="NW" name="Northwest"
/>
        <windSpeed mps="5.82" name="Moderate breeze" />
        <temperature unit="celsius" value="286.81" min="286.81"
max="287.573" />
        <pressure unit="hPa" value="1019.04" />
        <humidity value="63" unit="%" />
        <clouds value="clear sky" all="0" unit="%" />
    </time>
</forecast>
</weatherdata>
```

The DOM method

The first method of parsing the XML data will be using the **Document Object Model (DOM)**, which represents the structure of the XML document as a series of objects. The API to this is very similar to the API in JavaScript for manipulating HTML in the webpage.

We will start by setting the character encoding for the script. This is required as we will be using the degree symbol later in the script, and the UTF-8 encoding is required to display this character.

```
# -*- coding: utf-8 -*-
```

Next, we will continue by importing the modules that will be required for this script:

```
from datetime import datetime
import urllib2
from string import Template
import sys
import xml.dom.minidom
```

The following string template defines the format for the API URL that will be requested. This has a single substitution for the location of which to retrieve the forecast.

```
URL_TEMLATE =
Template('http://api.openweathermap.org/data/2.5/forecast?q=$
{location}&mode=xml')
```

Here, we retrieve the name of the location to search for from the command line and retrieve the XML document returned by the API as a string:

```
search_location = sys.argv[1]
api_url = URL_TEMLATE.substitute(location=search_location)
response = urllib2.urlopen(api_url)
xml_response = response.read()
```

Now, we will parse the XML as a DOM tree, which will allow us to search through the document to find certain data:

```
DOMTree = xml.dom.minidom.parseString(xml_response)
weather_data = DOMTree.documentElement
```

We will first search for the location details of the location that was actually used in retrieving the forecast (as there are cases where this can be different to the search text). To do this, we first retrieve the location block by selecting the first tag named `location`:

```
location = weather_data.getElementsByTagName('location')[0]
```

Next, we do the same process to retrieve the `name` and `country` tags, this time also taking the contents of the tag:

```
location_name =
location.getElementsByTagName('name')[0].childNodes[0].data
location_country =
location.getElementsByTagName('country')[0].childNodes[0].data
```

This line simply outputs the information to the terminal about the location used in the forecast:

```
print '5 day forecast for %s, %s.\n' % (location_name,
location_country)
```

Now, we loop over each of the `time` blocks in the `forecast` block of the XML document:

```
forecasts = weather_data.getElementsByTagName('time')
for forecast in forecasts:
```

Next, we extract the time this forecast is for — a string describing the overall weather conditions and the temperature:

```
api_time_string = forecast.getAttribute('from')
time = datetime.strptime(api_time_string, '%Y-%m-
%dT%H:%M:%S')
time_string = datetime.strftime(time, '%H:%M %d %B')
overview = forecast.getElementsByTagName('symbol')[0]
overview_string = overview.getAttribute('name')
temperature = forecast.getElementsByTagName('temperature')[0]
temperature_string = '?'
if temperature.hasAttribute('value'):
    temperature_string = '%.1f' %
(float(temperature.getAttribute('value')) - 273.15)
```

Finally, we print a line to the terminal containing the weather conditions extracted from the XML:

```
print u'%s: %s, %s°C' % (
        time_string,
        overview_string,
        temperature_string)
```

You can type the degree symbol (°) by holding the *Alt* key and typing 248.

Once the script is completed, it can be saved as `weather_xml_dom.py` and executed with the following command:

python weather_xml_dom.py Harwell,UK

This will provide an output similar to that shown in the following screenshot:

```
dan@dannixon-envy-ubuntu ~/G/Chapter08 (book_release=)> python weather_xml_dom.py Harwell,UK
5 day forecast for Harwell, GB.

18:00 06 July: few clouds, 17.0°C
21:00 06 July: scattered clouds, 15.0°C
00:00 07 July: overcast clouds, 14.1°C
03:00 07 July: light rain, 15.8°C
06:00 07 July: light rain, 17.3°C
09:00 07 July: light rain, 18.8°C
12:00 07 July: light rain, 20.3°C
15:00 07 July: broken clouds, 17.5°C
18:00 07 July: light rain, 15.1°C
21:00 07 July: light rain, 14.0°C
00:00 08 July: light rain, 13.5°C
03:00 08 July: light rain, 14.1°C
06:00 08 July: light rain, 16.3°C
09:00 08 July: broken clouds, 18.2°C
```

The SAX method

In this example, we will recreate the weather utility that, we created using the DOM method of parsing XML, but instead, here, we will use the **Simple API for XML (SAX)** method. The main difference is that DOM represents the entire document, whereas SAX operates over smaller sections of the document as it is read. Since it does not require the entire document to be read before it can be parsed by the application, the SAX method is much more memory efficient than DOM for parsing larger XML documents.

The start of this script will be very similar to that of the DOM example, the only difference being the XML parsing libraries:

```
# -*- coding: utf-8 -*-
from datetime import datetime
import urllib2
import xml.sax
from string import Template
import sys
```

Using the SAX method, we must create a class that will be used to handle the XML data as it is parsed from the string. This must inherit from the ContentHandler class provided by the xml.sax module.

```
class WeatherHandler(xml.sax.ContentHandler):
    def __init__(self):
        self._tag_buffer = list()
        self._location_name = '?'
        self._location_country = '?'
        self._time_string= ''
        self._overview_string = ''
        self._temperature_string = ''
```

The startElement function is called when a new element is detected in the XML document. Here, we are using it to record the current position in the document hierarchy using the _tag_buffer variable, and to record some of the data that is stored in the attributes:

```
    def startElement(self, tag, attributes):
        self._tag_buffer.append(tag)
        if self._tag_buffer[-2:] == ['weatherdata', 'location']:
            self._location_name = '?'
            self._location_country = '?'
        elif self._tag_buffer[-2:] == ['forecast', 'time']:
            time = datetime.strptime(attributes['from'], '%Y-%m-%dT%H:%M:%S')
```

```
                self._time_string = datetime.strftime(time, '%H:%M %d
  %B')
                self._overview_string = '?'
                self._temperature_string = '?'
           elif self._tag_buffer[-2:] == ['time', 'symbol']:
               if 'name' in attributes:
                   self._overview_string = attributes['name']
           elif self._tag_buffer[-2:] == ['time', 'temperature']:
               if 'value' in attributes:
                   self._temperature_string = '%.1f' %
  (float(attributes['value']) - 273.15)
```

The endElement function is called when an element is closed. Here, we are using it to update the position in the hierarchy by removing the last entry in the _tag_buffer variable and printing information to the terminal based on the type of tag that was closed:

```
      def endElement(self, tag):
          if self._tag_buffer[-2:] == ['weatherdata', 'location']:
              print '5 day forecast for %s, %s.\n' % (self._location_
  name, self._location_country)
          elif self._tag_buffer[-2:] == ['forecast', 'time']:
              print u'%s: %s, %s°C' % (
                      self._time_string,
                      self._overview_string,
                      self._temperature_string)
          self._tag_buffer.pop()
```

The characters function is called when the contents of a tag are read. It is used to record the location information in our parser.

```
      def characters(self, content):
          if self._tag_buffer[-2:] == ['location', 'name']:
              self._location_name = content
          elif self._tag_buffer[-2:] == ['location', 'country']:
              self._location_country = content
```

The following section of the code is identical to that used in the script with the DOM method:

```
URL_TEMLATE =
Template('http://api.openweathermap.org/data/2.5/forecast?q=$
{location}&mode=xml')
search_location = sys.argv[1]
api_url = URL_TEMLATE.substitute(location=search_location)
response = urllib2.urlopen(api_url)
xml_response = response.read()
```

Now, we will use the content handler class we just created to parse the XML string:

```
content_handler = WeatherHandler()
xml.sax.parseString(xml_response, content_handler)
```

Once the script is complete, save it as `weather_xml_sax.py`, and it can be executed using the following command:

python weather_xml_sax.py Harwell,UK

This will provide an output similar to that shown in the following screenshot:

```
dan@dannixon-envy-ubuntu ~/G/Chapter08 (book_release=)> python weather_xml_sax.py Harwell,UK
5 day forecast for Harwell, GB.

18:00 06 July: few clouds, 17.0°C
21:00 06 July: scattered clouds, 15.0°C
00:00 07 July: overcast clouds, 14.1°C
03:00 07 July: light rain, 15.8°C
06:00 07 July: light rain, 17.3°C
09:00 07 July: light rain, 18.8°C
12:00 07 July: light rain, 20.3°C
15:00 07 July: broken clouds, 17.5°C
18:00 07 July: light rain, 15.1°C
21:00 07 July: light rain, 14.0°C
00:00 08 July: light rain, 13.5°C
03:00 08 July: light rain, 14.1°C
06:00 08 July: light rain, 16.3°C
09:00 08 July: broken clouds, 18.2°C
```

Parsing a web page using BeautifulSoup

In this section, we will use the `BeautifulSoup` library to parse an HTML web page to extract information from it. This is particularly useful for when you wish to interact with a web page that does not provide an API to access their data, with the drawback being that it is more likely that an application using this method will be broken by a change in the web page structure (rather than an API, which is rarely changed, and when they are, developers are typically given warning of such a change).

In this next example, we will write a simple script to download low resolution previews of images from Pixiv (www.pixiv.net). This script will start in a similar way to the others we have written so far. Note that the UTF-8 character encoding is required here as the contents of the web pages are likely to contain Japanese characters.

```
# -*- coding: utf-8 -*-
from bs4 import BeautifulSoup
import urllib2
import os
import sys
from string import Template
```

This string template defines the URL for the page that allows unregistered users to view a preview of an image. Here, there is a substitution for the image ID (an 8 digit number).

```
URL_TEMPLATE =
Template('http://www.pixiv.net/member_illust.php?mode=
medium&illust_id=${illust_id}')
```

The following three lines download the contents of the web page, as has been used in the previous examples in this chapter:

```
pixiv_illust_id = sys.argv[1]
page_url = URL_TEMPLATE.substitute(illust_id=pixiv_illust_id)
response = urllib2.urlopen(page_url)
```

The following line parses the web page in order to allow us to search and read the document using the BeautifulSoup functions:

```
soup = BeautifulSoup(response.read())
```

Now that we have the web page searchable in BeautifulSoup, we need to find where we need to look in the document for the information we want to retrieve. We will start with the title of the image.

In order to find the location of such information in the HTML tree, it is worth opening the web page in a browser that allows you to show the relevant HTML source for a highlighted section of the page (I have used Google Chrome in the examples here).

The following image shows the image title being stored in an `h1` tag within a `div` tag of class `userdata`:

We can use `BeautifulSoup` to search for this data using the following two lines of code; the first line finds the `div` tag, and the second selects the first `h1` tag:

```
user_data = soup.find("div", {"class": "userdata"})
img_title = user_data.h1.contents[0]
```

The second piece of data that we will retrieve is the author of the image. We will use the web browser to search for this in the same way and find it to be in an h2 tag within the same div tag as the title, as shown in the following screenshot:

Since we already have the div tag as the image_data variable, retrieving the image author is a simple one line task:

```
img_author = user_data.h2.a.contents[0]
```

The final piece of information that we need to obtain is the URL from which we can download the low resolution version of the image. As is shown in the following screenshot, this is stored as the source of the image displayed in the div tag of the class img-container:

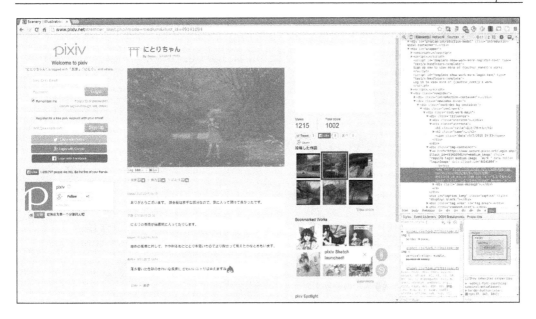

This information can be selected using the following line, which selects the src attribute from the img tag:

```
img_url = soup.find("div", {"class": "img-
container"}).a.img['src']
```

Now that we have all the information about the image, we can download it using urllib2, as we have previously done with plain text for web pages and APIs. Here, we are also attaching a header to the request before it is sent; in this case, this is to allow us to download the image, as a query without this header will fail:

```
print 'Downloading %s by %s' % (img_title, img_author)
img_request = urllib2.Request(img_url)
img_request.add_header('Referer', 'http://www.pixiv.net/')
img_data = urllib2.urlopen(img_request).read()
```

Finally, we will save the image to disk using Python's native file IO functions, which were covered in *Chapter 3, Working with Data Structures and I/O*. The first two lines here are used to determine the filename based on the title, the author retrieved from the web page, and the image extension of the image URL:

```
img_extension = os.path.splitext(img_url)[1][1:]
img_filename = '%s_%s.%s' % (img_author, img_title,
img_extension)
img_file = open(img_filename, 'wb')
img_file.write(img_data)
img_file.close()
print 'Saved as %s' % (img_filename)
```

When the script is complete, we can save the file as `pixiv_downloader.py`. Before we can run the script, we must first install the `BeautifulSoup` library using the following command:

sudo pip install beautifulsoup4

Now that we have all the required libraries installed, we can execute the script using the following command:

python pixiv_downloader.py 49141094

This will produce the following output on the terminal, and you will see the image file appear in the current directory:

```
dan@dannixon-envy-ubuntu ~/G/Chapter08 (book_release=)> python pixiv_downloader.py 49141094
Downloading にとりちゃん by SasaJ
Saved as SasaJ_にとりちゃん.jpg
```

Summary

In this chapter, we looked at the `urllib2` Python module and how this can be used to download data from the internet, as well as a series of modules and libraries for parsing the data in a variety of formats once it has been downloaded.

In the next chapter, we will start looking at building complete applications as we start designing and implementing command line interfaces.

9
Creating Command-line Interfaces

In this chapter, we will take a look at how we can use the `argparse` module to create easy to use **command line interfaces** (**CLIs**). CLIs can provide a much easier way to develop interface for your applications and are appropriate for situations where a graphical interface is not necessarily required.

To demonstrate the use of the module, we will build a simple unit conversion application that allows the user to input a value in a given unit and have the program convert it to a set of different units.

Unit conversion application

Before we can design the command line interface, we need to build up the framework for the unit conversion application. A rough structure of this application is shown in the following UML diagram:

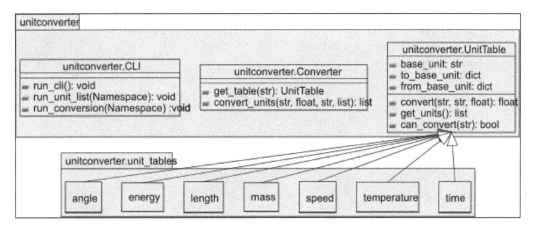

Note that because the unit conversion portion of this application is not the main focus here, not all the code for the unit conversions will be listed. However, they are available with the code download for this chapter.

The UnitTable class contains functions that convert between the units by first converting to a common base unit. To do this, there are two dictionaries with conversion steps for each unit supported by the table: one to convert to **from the base unit** and one to convert **to the base unit**.

Additional tables are created by inheriting from the UnitTable class and adding new entries to the to_base_unit and from_base_unit dictionaries. Note that every unit in a unit table must be able to convert to and from the base unit.

We will start by using the existing unit conversion framework by copying the unitconverter directory from the code provided for this chapter to a directory on the Pi and removing the CLI.py file for the time being.

Once the Python files are in place for the application, we can add a setup.py file that will be used to package the code. For now, this will include only the code to include the unit conversion utility as a library.

```python
from setuptools import setup
setup(
    name='unitconverter',
    version='0.1.0',
    description='Command line tool for unit conversion',
    classifiers=[
    'Natural Language :: English',
    'Programming Language :: Python :: 2.7',
    ],
    author='Dan Nixon',
    packages=['unitconverter', 'unitconverter.unit_tables'],
    include_package_data=True,
    zip_safe=False)
```

At this point, the code in the directory should follow the structure shown in the following screenshot:

```
dan@dannixon-envy-ubuntu ~/G/Chapter09 (book_release=)> tree .
.
├── setup.py
└── unitconverter
    ├── Converter.py
    ├── __init__.py
    ├── UnitTable.py
    └── unit_tables
        ├── angle.py
        ├── energy.py
        ├── __init__.py
        ├── length.py
        ├── mass.py
        ├── speed.py
        ├── temperature.py
        └── time.py
```

This will install the unitconverter package so that it can be included in any Python code we write. To demonstrate this, we can first install the module using the following command:

```
sudo python setup.py install
```

This command will give an output similar to that shown in the following screenshot:

```
removing 'build/bdist.linux-x86_64/egg' (and everything under it)
Processing unitconverter-0.1.0-py2.7.egg
removing '/usr/local/lib/python2.7/dist-packages/unitconverter-0.1.0-py2.7.egg' (and everything under it)
creating /usr/local/lib/python2.7/dist-packages/unitconverter-0.1.0-py2.7.egg
Extracting unitconverter-0.1.0-py2.7.egg to /usr/local/lib/python2.7/dist-packages
unitconverter 0.1.0 is already the active version in easy-install.pth
Installing unitconvert script to /usr/local/bin

Installed /usr/local/lib/python2.7/dist-packages/unitconverter-0.1.0-py2.7.egg
Processing dependencies for unitconverter==0.1.0
Finished processing dependencies for unitconverter==0.1.0
dan@dannixon-envy-ubuntu ~/G/Chapter09 (book_release=)>
```

Once the module is installed, we can demonstrate its use using the interactive Python terminal, using the following script:

```python
from unitconverter.Converter import get_table, convert_units
get_table('time').get_units()
convert_units('energy', 200, 'wh', ['j', 'hph'])
```

Here, the first line simply imports functions from the unit conversion library, the second line returns a list of all the units the energy unit table is capable of converting, and the third line converts 200 Watt-hours to Joules and horsepower-hours.

The output of this script is shown in the following screenshot:

```
dan@dannixon-envy-ubuntu ~> python
Python 2.7.6 (default, Mar 22 2014, 22:59:56)
[GCC 4.8.2] on linux2
Type "help", "copyright", "credits" or "license" for more information.
>>> from unitconverter.Converter import get_table, convert_units
>>> get_table('time').get_units()
set(['d', 'h', 'm', 'us', 's', 'ms', 'y', 'ns'])
>>> convert_units('energy', 200, 'wh', ['j', 'hph'])
[{'dest_unit': 'j', 'converted_value': 719999.99999424}, {'dest_unit': 'hph', 'converted_value': 0.2682044216834544}]
>>>
```

Command-line interface

Now that the framework for the unit conversion is complete, we can start work on the command line interface, used to form the full application.

We will expand the application to include a command line interface by creating a new file named CLI.py in the unitconverter directory. We will start this file by including the required modules and functions:

```
import argparse
import inspect
from Converter import get_table, convert_units
```

The run_cli() function is going to be called whenever the unit conversion application is invoked from the command line. It is responsible for parsing the input from the command line and performing the required conversions. This starts by creating a ArgumentParser object, to which we can add arguments that are to be parsed from the command line:

```
def run_cli():
    parser = argparse.ArgumentParser(description='Tool for
converting units')
```

The first argument will be used to define the conversion table that will be used in the unit conversion:

```
parser.add_argument(
    'table',
    metavar='TABLE',
    action='store',
    type=str,
```

```
        help='Unit table to use in conversion'
    )
```

We will now create two subparsers: one for unit conversion mode and another for listing the units that are supported by a given unit table. The set_defaults function is used to set the default values for a subparser. In this case, we are using it to provide a method of determining which subparser was used:

```
subparsers = parser.add_subparsers(help='operation to be
performed')
list_table_parser = subparsers.add_parser('list')
list_table_parser.set_defaults(which='list')
conversion_parser = subparsers.add_parser('convert')
conversion_parser.set_defaults(which='convert')
```

Next, we will add an optional argument for the subparser for the mode to list all the possible conversions. This argument, when provided, will also output the formula that converts the base unit to each given formula.

```
list_table_parser.add_argument(
    '-m', '--method',
    action='store_true',
    help='Also output the conversion method from the base
unit'
    )
```

We will now add positional requirements to the subparser for unit conversion mode, which will be used to parse the original value, the unit it is in, and a list of the units to convert to:

```
conversion_parser.add_argument(
    'value',
    metavar='VALUE',
    type=float,
    action='store',
    help='The value to convert'
)
conversion_parser.add_argument(
    'from_unit',
    metavar='FROM',
    action='store',
    type=str,
    help='Unit to convert from'
)
conversion_parser.add_argument(
    'to_units',
```

```
        metavar='TO',
        action='store',
        nargs='+',
        type=str,
        help='Unit(s) to convert to'
    )
```

The next step is to call the `parse_args` function to parse the options from the command line. This will return a Python namespace containing the options that have been retrieved.

```
props = parser.parse_args()
```

Next, depending on whether the script was invoked in the unit conversion or the listing mode, we will run either the `_run_unit_list` or `_run_conversion` function to perform the processing of the application:

```
if props.which == 'list':
    _run_unit_list(props)
elif props.which == 'convert':
    _run_conversion(props)
```

This function is used when the application is invoked in the listing mode. In this mode, all the units in a given unit table are printed to the terminal, optionally if the `-m` parameter is given, then the formula used to convert from the base unit to each unit will also be given.

```
def _run_unit_list(props):
    table = get_table(props.table)
    print 'Unit table %s can convert between the units:'
    for unit in table.get_units():
        if props.method:
            if unit == table.base_unit:
                formula = 'base unit'
            else:
```

This code is responsible for retrieving the formula used in the lambda that performs the unit conversion from the base unit to the current unit being printed. This is done using the `inspect` module, which can be used to retrieve the source code for Python types.

```
                conversion = inspect.getsource(table.from_base_
unit[unit])
                formula = conversion[conversion.
index(':')+1:conversion.index('\n')].strip(
)
```

```
        print '%s (%s)' % (unit, formula)
    else:
        print unit
```

This function is used to run the application in the unit conversion mode. Here, it uses the functions in the `Converter` module to perform the conversion and prints the results to the terminal.

```
def _run_conversion(props):
    results = convert_units(table_name=props.table,
                            value=props.value,
                            value_unit=props.from_unit,
                            targets=props.to_units)
    for result in results:
        print '%f %s = %f %s' % (props.value, props.from_unit,
                                 result['converted_value'],
                                 result['dest_unit'])
```

At this point, the code structure should be as shown in the following image:

The next step is to add the console entry point to the `setup.py` file so that the command is registered when the package is installed. The following code should be added under the line containing `version`:

```
entry_points = {
    'console_scripts': ['unitconvert=unitconverter.CLI:run_cli'],
},
```

Next, run the following command once again to install the package; this time also installing the command line interface files:

```
sudo python setup.py install
```

Now that the application is installed, it can be executed using the `unitconvert` command on the shell. An example of this showing the units of energy that can be converted is given as follows:

```
unitconvert energy list
```

This gives the output shown in the following screenshot:

```
dan@dannixon-envy-ubuntu ~> unitconvert energy list
Unit table %s can convert between the units:
btu
j
wh
hph
cal
ev
kcal
```

The same command can also be used with the `-m` argument as shown next, which also outputs the conversion formula:

```
unitconvert energy list -m
```

This gives the output shown in the following screenshot:

```
dan@dannixon-envy-ubuntu ~> unitconvert energy list -m
Unit table %s can convert between the units:
btu (x * 0.00094781707775)
j (base unit)
wh (x * 0.00027777777778)
hph (x * 3.7250614123e-7)
cal (x * 0.23900573614)
ev (x * 6241506480000000000.0)
kcal (x * 0.00023884589663)
```

The application can be used to perform a unit conversion by providing the original value, its unit, and a list of the units to convert to. For example, to convert 2500 kilocalories (or nutritional calories) to Calories, Joules, and electron volts, the following command would be used:

```
unitconvert energy convert 2500 kcal cal j ev
```

This gives the output shown in the following screenshot:

```
dan@dannixon-envy-ubuntu ~> unitconvert energy convert 2500 kcal cal j ev
2500.000000 kcal = 2501673.040151 cal
2500.000000 kcal = 10466999.999890 j
2500.000000 kcal = 6532984832547508069597184O.000000 ev
```

Summary

In this chapter, we looked at how the `argparse` Python module can be used to create command line interfaces around applications.

In the next chapter, we will look at the ways in which we can troubleshoot the Python code we write, and design applications to be easily debugged by having them write log files.

10
Debugging Applications with PDB and Log Files

In this chapter, we will learn more about how to debug Python code using the **Python Debugger** (**PDB**) tool and how we can use the Python logging framework to make complex applications written in Python easier to debug when they fail.

We will also look at the technique of unit testing and how the `unittest` Python module can be used to test small sections of a Python application to ensure that it is functioning as expected.

These techniques are commonly used in applications written in other languages and are good skills to learn if you are often going to be developing applications.

We will be making additions to the calculator application developed in *Chapter 4, Understanding Object-oriented Programming and Threading*; a copy of the code for this is included in the code for this chapter.

The Python debugger

PDB is a tool that allows real time debugging of running Python code. It can help to track down issues with the logic of a program to help find the cause of a crash or unexpected behavior.

PDB can be launched with the following command:

```
pdb2.7 do_calculaton.py
```

This will open a new PDB shell, as shown in the following screenshot:

```
dan@dannixon-envy-ubuntu ~/G/C/calculator (book_release=)> pdb2.7 do_calculation.py
> /home/dan/GettingStartedWithPythonAndRaspberyPi/Chapter10/calculator/do_calculation.py(3)<module>()
-> from Calculator import Calculator
(Pdb)
```

We can use the continue command (which can be shortened to c) to execute the next section of the code until a breakpoint is hit. As we are yet to declare any breakpoints, this will run the script until it exits normally, as shown in the following screenshot:

```
(Pdb) c
2.5
The program finished and will be restarted
> /home/dan/GettingStartedWithPythonAndRaspberyPi/Chapter10/calculator/do_calculation.py(3)<module>()
-> from Calculator import Calculator
(Pdb)
```

We can set breakpoints in the application, where the program will be stopped, and you will be taken back to the PDB shell in order to debug the control flow of the program. The easiest way to set a breakpoint is by giving a specific line in a file, for example:

break Operation.py:7

This command will add a breakpoint on line 7 of Operation.py. When this is added, PDB will confirm the file and the line number, as shown in the following screenshot:

```
(Pdb) break Operation.py:7
Breakpoint 1 at /home/dan/GettingStartedWithPythonAndRaspberyPi/Chapter10/calculator/Operation.py:7
(Pdb)
```

Now, when we run the application, we will see the program stop each time the breakpoint is reached. When a breakpoint is reached, we can resume the program using the c command:

```
(Pdb) c
> /home/dan/GettingStartedWithPythonAndRaspberyPi/Chapter10/calculator/Operation.py(7)__init__()
-> self._operation = name
(Pdb)
```

When paused at a breakpoint, we can view the details of the local variables in the current scope. For example, in the breakpoint we have added, there is a variable named name, which we can see the value of by using the following command:

p name

This outputs the value of the variable, as shown in the following screenshot:

```
(Pdb) p name
'add'
(Pdb) 
```

When at a breakpoint, we can also get a stack trace of the functions that have been called so far. This is done using the `bt` command and gives output like that shown in the following screenshot:

```
(Pdb) bt
  /usr/lib/python2.7/bdb.py(400)run()
-> exec cmd in globals, locals
  <string>(1)<module>()
  /home/dan/GettingStartedWithPythonAndRaspberyPi/Chapter10/calculator/do_calculation.py(8)<module>()
-> c.enter_operation("add")
  /home/dan/GettingStartedWithPythonAndRaspberyPi/Chapter10/calculator/Calculator.py(19)enter_operation()
-> self._input_list.append(Operation(operation_name))
> /home/dan/GettingStartedWithPythonAndRaspberyPi/Chapter10/calculator/Operation.py(7)__init__()
-> self._operation = name
(Pdb) 
```

We can also modify the values of the variables when paused at a breakpoint. To do this, simply assign a value to the variable name as you would in a regular Python script:

```
name = 'subtract'
```

In the following screenshot, this was used to change the first operation in the `do_calculation.py` script from add to subtract; the effect on the calculation is seen in the different result value:

```
(Pdb) name = 'subtract'
(Pdb) p name
'subtract'
(Pdb) c
> /home/dan/GettingStartedWithPythonAndRaspberyPi/Chapter10/calculator/Operation.py(7)__init__()
-> self._operation = name
(Pdb) c
> /home/dan/GettingStartedWithPythonAndRaspberyPi/Chapter10/calculator/Operation.py(7)__init__()
-> self._operation = name
(Pdb) c
-2.0
The program finished and will be restarted
> /home/dan/GettingStartedWithPythonAndRaspberyPi/Chapter10/calculator/do_calculation.py(3)<module>()
-> from Calculator import Calculator
(Pdb) 
```

When at a breakpoint, we can also use the l command to see the current line the program is paused at. An example of this is shown in the following screenshot:

```
(Pdb) l
 14 B            self._input_list.append(float(value))
 15
 16        def enter_operation(self, operation_name):
 17            if len(self._input_list) == 0 or isinstance(self._input_list[-1], Operation):
 18                raise RuntimeError("Must enter a value next")
 19 B->         self._input_list.append(Operation(operation_name))
 20
 21        def evaluate(self):
 22            self._result = self._input_list[0]
 23            for idx in range(1, len(self._input_list), 2):
 24                operation = self._input_list[idx]
(Pdb)
```

We can also setup a series of commands to be executed when we hit a breakpoint. This can allow debugging to be automated to an extent by automatically recording or modifying the values of the variables at certain points in the program's execution.

This can be demonstrated using the following commands on a new instance of PDB with no breakpoints set (first, quit PDB using the q command, and then re-launch it):

break Operation.py:7

commands

p name

c

This gives the following output. Note that the commands are entered on a terminal prefixed (com) rather than the PDB terminal prefixed (pdb).

```
(Pdb) break Operation.py:7
Breakpoint 1 at /home/dan/GettingStartedWithPythonAndRaspberyPi/Chapter10/calculator/Operation.py:7
(Pdb) commands
(com) print name
(com) c
(Pdb)
```

This set of commands tells PDB to print the value of the name variable and continue execution when the last added breakpoint was hit. This gives the output shown in the following screenshot:

```
(Pdb) c
add
> /home/dan/GettingStartedWithPythonAndRaspberyPi/Chapter10/calculator/Operation.py(7)__init__()
-> self._operation = name
multiply
> /home/dan/GettingStartedWithPythonAndRaspberyPi/Chapter10/calculator/Operation.py(7)__init__()
-> self._operation = name
divide
> /home/dan/GettingStartedWithPythonAndRaspberyPi/Chapter10/calculator/Operation.py(7)__init__()
-> self._operation = name
2.5
The program finished and will be restarted
> /home/dan/GettingStartedWithPythonAndRaspberyPi/Chapter10/calculator/do_calculation.py(3)<module>()
-> from Calculator import Calculator
(Pdb)
```

Within PDB, you can also use the ? command to get a full list of the available commands and help on using them, as shown in the following screenshot:

```
(Pdb) ?

Documented commands (type help <topic>):
========================================
EOF     bt          cont      enable  jump  pp       run       unt
a       c           continue  exit    l     q        s         until
alias   cl          d         h       list  quit     step      up
args    clear       debug     help    n     r        tbreak    w
b       commands    disable   ignore  next  restart  u         whatis
break   condition   down      j       p     return   unalias   where

Miscellaneous help topics:
==========================
exec  pdb

Undocumented commands:
======================
retval  rv
```

Further information and full documentation on PDB is available at https://docs.python.org/2/library/pdb.html.

Writing log files

The next technique we will look at is having our application output a log file. This allows us to get a better understanding of what was happening at the time an application failed, which can provide key information into finding the cause of the failure, especially when the failure is being reported by a user of your application.

We will add some logging statements to the Calculator.py and Operation.py files. To do this, we must first add the import for the logging module (https://docs.python.org/2/library/logging.html) to the start of each python file, which is simply:

```
import logging
```

In the Operation.py file, we will add two logging calls in the evaluate function, as shown in the following code:

```
def evaluate(self, a, b):
    logging.getLogger(__name__).info("Evaluating operation: %s" %
(self._operation))
    logging.getLogger(__name__).debug("RHS: %f, LHS: %f" % (a, b))
```

This will output two logging statements: one at the debug level and one at the information level. There are in total five unique levels at which messages can be output. In increasing severity, they are:

- debug()
- info()
- warning()
- error()
- critical()

Log handlers can be filtered to only process the log messages of a certain severity if required. We will see this in action later in this section.

The logging.getLogger(__name__) call is used to retrieve the Logger class for the current module (where the name of the module is given by the __name__ variable). By default, each module uses its own Logger class identified by the name of the module.

Next, we can add some debugging statements to the Calculator.py file in the same way. Here, we will add logging to the enter_value, enter_operation, evaluate, and all_clear functions, as shown in the following code snippet:

```
def enter_value(self, value):
    if len(self._input_list) > 0 and not isinstance(self._input_list[-
1], Operation):
```

```
            raise RuntimeError("Must enter an operation next")
        logging.getLogger(__name__).info("Adding value: %f" % (value))
        self._input_list.append(float(value))

    def enter_operation(self, operation_name):
        if len(self._input_list) == 0 or isinstance
(self._input_list[-1], Operation):
            raise RuntimeError("Must enter a value next")
        logging.getLogger(__name__).info("Adding operation: %s" %
(operation_name))
        self._input_list.append(Operation(operation_name))

    def evaluate(self):
        logging.getLogger(__name__).info("Evaluating calculation")
        if len(self._input_list) % 2 == 0:
            raise RuntimeError("Input length mismatch")
        self._result = self._input_list[0]
        for idx in range(1, len(self._input_list), 2):
            operation = self._input_list[idx]
            next_value = self._input_list[idx + 1]
            logging.getLogger(__name__).debug
("Next function: %f %s %f" % (
                self._result, str(operation), next_value))
            self._result = operation.evaluate
(self._result, next_value)
        logging.getLogger(__name__).info
("Result is: %f" % (self._result))
        return self._result

    def all_clear(self):
        logging.getLogger(__name__).info("Clearing calculator")
        self._input_list = []
        self._result = 0.0
```

Finally, we need to configure a handler for the log messages. This is what will handle the messages sent by each logger and output them to a suitable destination; for example, the standard output or a file.

We will configure this in the do_conversion.py file. First, we will configure a basic handler that will print all the log messages to the standard output so that they appear on the terminal. This can be achieved with the following code:

```
logging.basicConfig(level=logging.DEBUG)
```

We will also add the following line to the end of the script. This is used to close any open log handlers and should be included at the very end of an application (the logging framework should not be used after calling this function).

```
logging.shutdown()
```

Now, we can see the effects by running the script using the following command:

python do_calculation.py

This will give an output to the terminal, as shown in the following screenshot:

```
dan@dannixon-envy-ubuntu ~/G/C/c/calculator (book_release=)> python do_calculation.py
INFO:Calculator:Adding value: 1.000000
INFO:Calculator:Adding operation: add
INFO:Calculator:Adding value: 9.000000
INFO:Calculator:Adding operation: multiply
INFO:Calculator:Adding value: 5.000000
INFO:Calculator:Adding operation: divide
INFO:Calculator:Adding value: 20.000000
INFO:Calculator:Evaluating calculation
DEBUG:Calculator:Next function: 1.000000 add 9.000000
INFO:Operation:Evaluating operation: add
DEBUG:Operation:RHS: 1.000000, LHS: 9.000000
DEBUG:Calculator:Next function: 10.000000 multiply 5.000000
INFO:Operation:Evaluating operation: multiply
DEBUG:Operation:RHS: 10.000000, LHS: 5.000000
DEBUG:Calculator:Next function: 50.000000 divide 20.000000
INFO:Operation:Evaluating operation: divide
DEBUG:Operation:RHS: 50.000000, LHS: 20.000000
INFO:Calculator:Result is: 2.500000
2.5
INFO:Calculator:Clearing calculator
```

We can also have the log output written to a file instead of printed to the terminal by adding a filename to the logger configuration. This helps to keep the terminal free of unnecessary information.

```
logging.basicConfig(level=logging.DEBUG, filename='calc.log')
```

When executed, this will give no additional output other than the result of the calculation, but will have created an additional file, `calc.log`, which contains the log messages, as shown in the following screenshot:

```
dan@dannixon-envy-ubuntu ~/G/C/c/calculator (book_release=)> python do_calculation.py
2.5
dan@dannixon-envy-ubuntu ~/G/C/c/calculator (book_release=)> cat calc.log
INFO:Calculator:Adding value: 1.000000
INFO:Calculator:Adding operation: add
INFO:Calculator:Adding value: 9.000000
INFO:Calculator:Adding operation: multiply
INFO:Calculator:Adding value: 5.000000
INFO:Calculator:Adding operation: divide
INFO:Calculator:Adding value: 20.000000
INFO:Calculator:Evaluating calculation
DEBUG:Calculator:Next function: 1.000000 add 9.000000
INFO:Operation:Evaluating operation: add
DEBUG:Operation:RHS: 1.000000, LHS: 9.000000
DEBUG:Calculator:Next function: 10.000000 multiply 5.000000
INFO:Operation:Evaluating operation: multiply
DEBUG:Operation:RHS: 10.000000, LHS: 5.000000
DEBUG:Calculator:Next function: 50.000000 divide 20.000000
INFO:Operation:Evaluating operation: divide
DEBUG:Operation:RHS: 50.000000, LHS: 20.000000
INFO:Calculator:Result is: 2.500000
INFO:Calculator:Clearing calculator
```

Unit testing

Unit testing is a technique for automated testing of small sections ("units") of code to ensure that the components of a larger application are working as intended, independently of each other.

There are many frameworks for this in almost every language. In Python, we will be using the `unittest` module, as this is included with the language and is the most common framework used in the Python applications.

To add unit tests to our calculator module, we will create an additional module in the same directory named `test`. Inside that will be three files: `__init__.py` (used to denote that a directory is a Python package), `test_Calculator.py`, and `test_Operation.py`.

After creating this additional module, the structure of the code will be the same as shown in the following image:

```
├── calculator
│   ├── Calculator.py
│   ├── do_calculation.py
│   ├── __init__.py
│   └── Operation.py
└── test
    ├── __init__.py
    ├── test_Calculator.py
    └── test_Operation.py

2 directories, 7 files
```

Next, we will modify the `test_Operation.py` file to include a test case for the `Operation` class. As always, this will start with the required imports for the modules we will be using:

```
import unittest
from calculator.Operation import Operation
```

We will be creating a class, `test_Operation`, which inherits from the `TestCase` class provided by the `unittest` module. This contains the logic required to run the functions of the class as individual unit tests.

```
class test_Operation(unittest.TestCase):
```

Now, we will define four tests to test the creation of a new `Operation` instance for each of the operations that are supported by the class. Here, the `assertEquals` function is used to test for equality between two variables; this determines if the test passes or not.

```
def test_create_add(self):
    op = Operation('add')
    self.assertEqual(str(op), 'add')

def test_create_subtract(self):
    op = Operation('subtract')
    self.assertEqual(str(op), 'subtract')

def test_create_multiply(self):
    op = Operation('multiply')
    self.assertEqual(str(op), 'multiply')
```

```
def test_create_divide(self):
    op = Operation('divide')
    self.assertEqual(str(op), 'divide')
```

In this test we are checking that a `RuntimeError` is raised when an unknown operation is given to the `Operation` constructor. We will do this using the `assertRaises` function.

```
def test_create_fails(self):
    self.assertRaises(ValueError,
                      Operation,
                      'not_a_function')
```

Next, we will create four tests to ensure that each of the known operations evaluates to the correct result:

```
def test_add(self):
    op = Operation('add')
    result = op.evaluate(5, 2)
    self.assertEqual(result, 7)

def test_subtract(self):
    op = Operation('subtract')
    result = op.evaluate(5, 2)
    self.assertEqual(result, 3)

def test_multiply(self):
    op = Operation('multiply')
    result = op.evaluate(5, 2)
    self.assertEqual(result, 10)

def test_divide(self):
    op = Operation('divide')
    result = op.evaluate(5, 2)
    self.assertEqual(result, 2)
```

This will form the test case for the `Operation` class. Typically, the test file for a module should have the name of the module prefixed by `test`, and the name of each test function within a test case class should start with `test`.

Next, we will create a test case for the `Calculator` class in the `test_Calculator.py` file. This again starts by importing the required modules and defining the class:

```
import unittest
from calculator.Calculator import Calculator
class test_Operation(unittest.TestCase):
```

We will now add two test cases that test the correct handling of errors when operations and values are entered in the incorrect order. This time, we will use the `assertRaises` function to create a context to test for `RuntimeError` being raised. In this case, the error must be raised by any of the code within the context.

```
def test_add_value_out_of_order_fails(self):
    with self.assertRaises(RuntimeError):
        calc = Calculator()
        calc.enter_value(5)
        calc.enter_value(5)
        calc.evaluate()

def test_add_operation_out_of_order_fails(self):
    with self.assertRaises(RuntimeError):
        calc = Calculator()
        calc.enter_operation('add')
        calc.evaluate()
```

This test is to ensure that the `all_clear` function works as expected. Note that, here, we have multiple test assertions in the function, and all assertions have to pass for the test to pass.

```
def test_all_clear(self):
    calc = Calculator()
    calc.enter_value(5)
    calc.evaluate()
    self.assertEqual(calc.get_result(), 5)
    calc.all_clear()
    self.assertEqual(calc.get_result(), 0)
```

This test ensured that the `evaluate()` function works as expected and checks the output of a known calculation. Note, here, that we are using the `assertAlmostEqual` function, which ensures that two numerical variables are equal within a given tolerance, in this case 13 decimal places.

```
def test_evaluate(self):
    calc = Calculator()
    calc.enter_value(5.0)
```

```
calc.enter_operation('multiply')
calc.enter_value(2.0)
calc.enter_operation('divide')
calc.enter_value(5.0)
calc.enter_operation('add')
calc.enter_value(18.0)
calc.enter_operation('subtract')
calc.enter_value(5.0)
self.assertAlmostEqual(calc.evaluate(), 15.0, 13)
self.assertAlmostEqual(calc.get_result(), 15.0, 13)
```

These two tests will test that the errors are handled correctly when the `evaluate()` function is called, when there are values missing from the input or the input is empty:

```
def test_evaluate_failure_empty(self):
    with self.assertRaises(RuntimeError):
        calc = Calculator()
        calc.enter_operation('add')
        calc.evaluate()

def test_evaluate_failure_missing_value(self):
    with self.assertRaises(RuntimeError):
        calc = Calculator()
        calc.enter_value(5)
        calc.enter_operation('add')
        calc.evaluate()
```

That completes the test case for the `Calculator` class.

Note that we have only used a small subset of the available test assertions over our two test classes. A full list of all the test assertions is available in the `unittest` module documentation at `https://docs.python.org/2/library/unittest.html#test-cases`.

Once all the tests are written, they can be executed using the following command in the directory containing both the `calculator` and `tests` directories:

```
python -m unittest discover -v
```

Here, we have the unit test framework discover all the tests automatically (which is why following the expected naming convention of prefixing names with "test" is important). We also request verbose output with the -v parameter, which shows all the tests executed and their results, as shown in the following screenshot:

```
dan@dannixon-envy-ubuntu ~/G/C/calculator_with_logs_and_tests (book_release=)> python -m unittest discover -v
test_add_operation_out_of_order_fails (test.test_Calculator.test_Operation) ... ok
test_add_value_out_of_order_fails (test.test_Calculator.test_Operation) ... ok
test_all_clear (test.test_Calculator.test_Operation) ... ok
test_evaluate (test.test_Calculator.test_Operation) ... ok
test_evaluate_failure_empty (test.test_Calculator.test_Operation) ... ok
test_evaluate_failure_missing_value (test.test_Calculator.test_Operation) ... ok
test_add (test.test_Operation.test_Operation) ... ok
test_create_add (test.test_Operation.test_Operation) ... ok
test_create_divide (test.test_Operation.test_Operation) ... ok
test_create_fails (test.test_Operation.test_Operation) ... ok
test_create_multiply (test.test_Operation.test_Operation) ... ok
test_create_subtract (test.test_Operation.test_Operation) ... ok
test_divide (test.test_Operation.test_Operation) ... ok
test_multiply (test.test_Operation.test_Operation) ... ok
test_subtract (test.test_Operation.test_Operation) ... ok

----------------------------------------------------------------------
Ran 15 tests in 0.001s

OK
```

Summary

In this chapter, we looked at how the PDB tool can be used to find faults in Python code and applications. We also looked at using the logging module to have Python code output a log file during execution and how this can make debugging the failures easier, as well as automated unit testing for portions of the application.

In the next chapter, we will look at the Qt GUI framework and how it can be used to create a graphical interface for a Python application.

11
Designing Your GUI with Qt

In this chapter, we will look at using the Qt (www.qt.io) framework to build a graphical interface for a Python application. In this case, we will be extending the unit conversion application created in *Chapter 9, Creating Command-line Interfaces*.

The Qt framework is a commonly used framework for a lot of open source desktop applications. It is written in C++ and, typically, most applications use the C++ Qt library. However, it also has a Python wrapper around this library, which is what we will use in this chapter.

Setting up the codebase

We will start extending the unit conversion application by taking a copy of the unitconverter directory and the setup.py scripts from the code written in *Chapter 9, Creating Command-line Interfaces* (a copy of this code is included in the code downloads for *Chapter 9, Creating Command-line Interfaces*).

We will then create a new module named gui within the unitconverter module. This will contain the Qt window that will provide a graphical interface to the unit conversion tool and the code that will launch it.

As we have done before, this is done by creating a directory named gui inside the unitconverter directory and a file named __init__.py inside the gui directory.

At this point, the code structure will be identical to that shown in the following image:

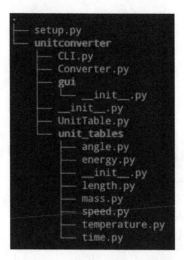

```
├── setup.py
└── unitconverter
    ├── CLI.py
    ├── Converter.py
    ├── gui
    │   └── __init__.py
    ├── __init__.py
    ├── UnitTable.py
    └── unit_tables
        ├── angle.py
        ├── energy.py
        ├── __init__.py
        ├── length.py
        ├── mass.py
        ├── speed.py
        ├── temperature.py
        └── time.py
```

We must also install the libraries and tools required to develop the application. This includes the `setuptools` utility for packaging Python code and the Qt framework and supporting utilities, including Qt Designer, which we will use later on to design the graphical portion of the user interface. These packages can be installed using the following command:

```
sudo apt-get install pyhon-setuptools python-qt4 qtcreator
```

Building the UI with Qt Designer

Start by launching Qt Designer using the following command:

```
designer-qt4
```

When Qt Designer first loads, you will see the **New Form** dialog box, as shown in the following screenshot:

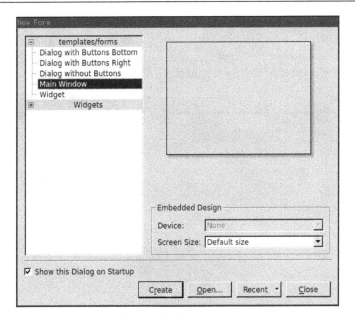

Here, select the **Main Window** option and click **Create**. You will then see the new window open in the main Qt Designer window, as follows:

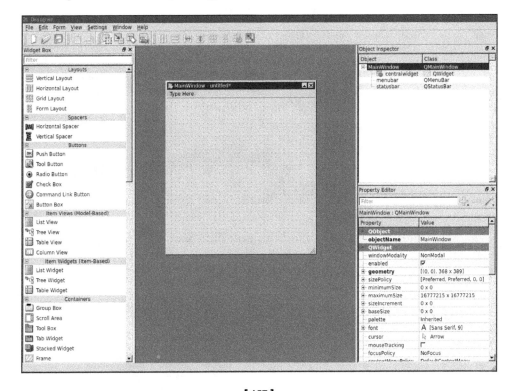

The first thing we need to do is to rename the window class name. This is done by first selecting **QMainWindow** in **Object Inspector**, and then changing the `objectName` property in **Property Editor** to `UnitConverter`. We will also change the `WindowTitle` property to "Unit Converter", as shown in the following screenshot:

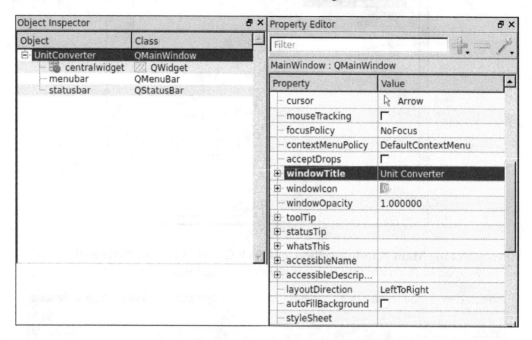

Next, we will add a menu to the top menu bar of the main window. This will only have a single File menu. To add this, click on the **Type Here** section in the position of the top menu bar and enter `&File`. Here, & is used to designate the character that can be used to access the menu using the *Alt* key.

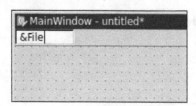

Add the option by pressing *Enter*, after which the menu should look similar to what is shown in the following screenshot:

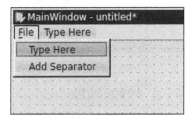

Next, we will add the Exit option to the **File** menu. This is done by clicking on the **File** menu to open it, and then clicking on the **Type Here** option within the menu. Here, type &Exit, as shown in the following screenshot:

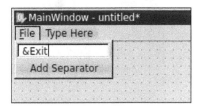

Again, add the option by pressing *Enter*. At this point, the menu should look similar to that shown in the following screenshot:

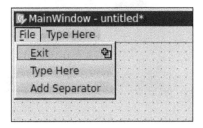

Next, we will add a widget to the window; this will be a Label widget, which can be found under the **Display Widgets** category of **Widget Box** to the left of Qt Designer. Drag a **Label** widget out of this box and onto the window. When the widget is dropped, the form should look something like the following screenshot:

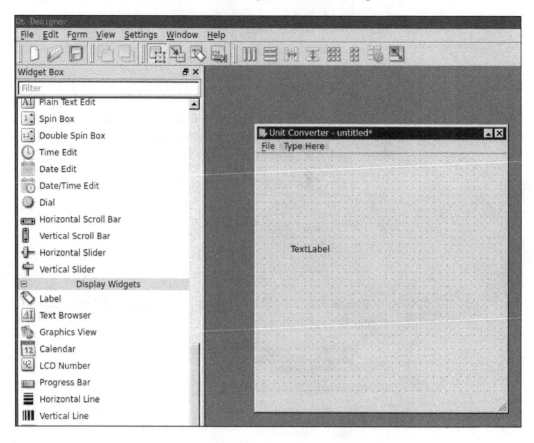

Now that the first widget has been added to the window, we can give the window a layout. In our case, we will be using the grid layout. This can be selected by right clicking in any empty space in the window and selecting **Lay out** and **Lay out in a Grid,** as shown in the following screenshot:

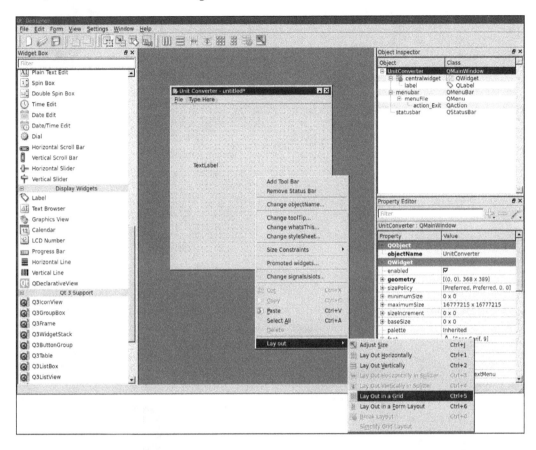

Now that the layout is set, we can add the remaining widgets. Next, we will add a ComboBox on the right hand side of the window opposite the label. This is again done by dragging the widget from **Widget Box** and dropping it in the position indicated in the following screenshot:

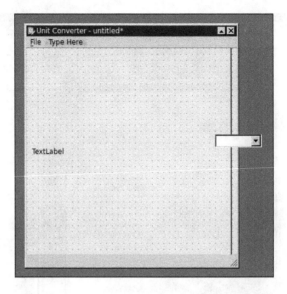

Next, we will add another Label widget underneath the first added one. As before, this is done by dragging it from **Widget Box** and dropping it in the position indicated as follows:

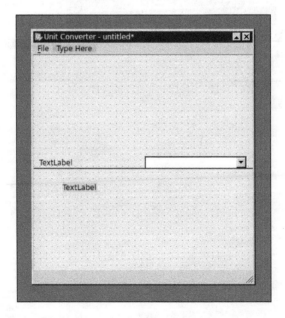

Now, we will add the remaining widgets. This should consist of five Label widgets in the left hand column of the grid layout and two ComboBox widgets, one DoubleSpinBox, another ComboBox, and a LineEdit widget (in that order) in the right hand column of the grid layout, as shown in the following screenshot:

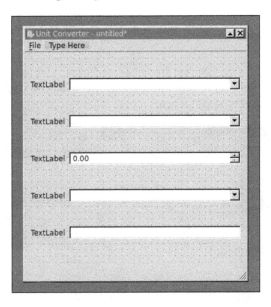

Next, we will edit the text displayed by the five Label widgets. This can be easily done by double clicking the widget in the window, as shown in the following screenshot:

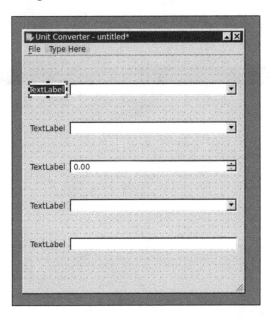

Here, the Label widgets from top to bottom should read as follows:

- **Unit Table:**
- **Source Unit:**
- **Value:**
- **Destination Unit:**
- **Value:**

Once all the Label widgets have been modified, the window should look similar to that shown in the following screenshot:

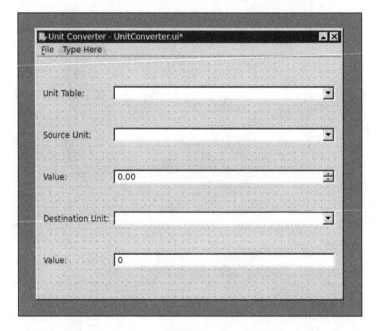

Next, we will resize the window so that it better accommodates the widgets that we have added. This can be done by dragging the bottom right hand corner of the window as you would resize any window.

Once complete, the window should look more like that shown in the following screenshot:

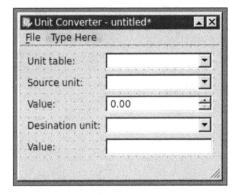

Now that all the widgets have been added, we will rename the widgets to more sensible names that reflect what they are actually used for in the user interface, which will be used later in the code to interact with the widget. Again, this is done by selecting the widget in the window and editing the `objectName` property in **Property Editor**, as shown in the following screenshot:

In our case, the names of the widgets from top to bottom, left to right, should be as follows:

- **lbUnitTable**
- **lbSourceUnit**
- **lbValue**
- **lbDestUnit**
- **lbDestValue**
- **cbUnitTable**
- **cbSourceUnit**
- **sbSourceValue**

- **cbDestUnit**
- **leDestValue**

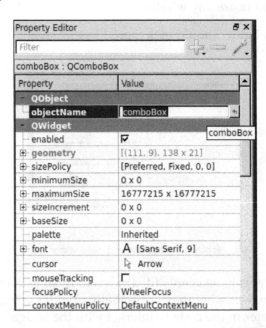

Once the widgets have been renamed, **Object Inspector** should look something similar to that shown in the following image:

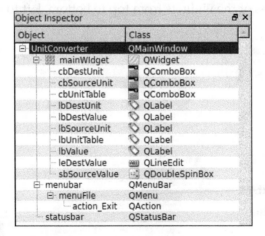

Next, we will disable the **LineEdit** widget that will be used for displaying the result of a unit conversion. This is done by selecting the widget and removing the tick in the **enabled** property in **Property Editor,** as shown in the following screenshot. This is to prevent the user from being able to change the result of the unit conversion.

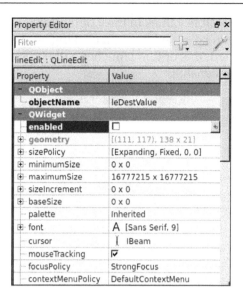

We will next increase the number of the decimal places and the range of values allowed in the DoubleSpinBox widget. Again, this is done via **Property Editor** after first selecting the widget.

Here, we will set the **decimals** property to 5 and increase the range of valid values to -9999 to 9999 using the **minimum** and **maximum** properties.

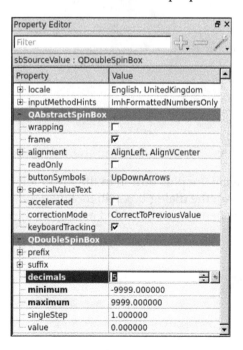

Now, we will enter the possible values in the ComboBox widget used to select the unit table. These values can be edited by right clicking on the widget and selecting **Edit Items...**. When selected, this option launches a dialog box similar to the one shown in the following screenshot:

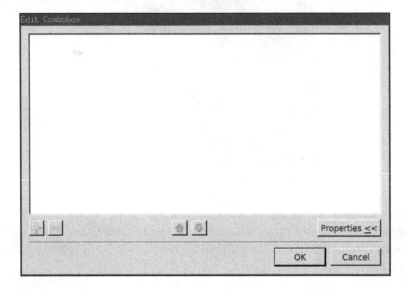

Here, we will add the following options to the widget:

- **angle**
- **energy**
- **length**
- **mass**
- **speed**
- **temperature**
- **time**

New items are added using the plus button in the lower left of the dialog. Once all the items have been added, the dialog box will look like that shown in the following screenshot. Note that the items must be added exactly as they are listed here.

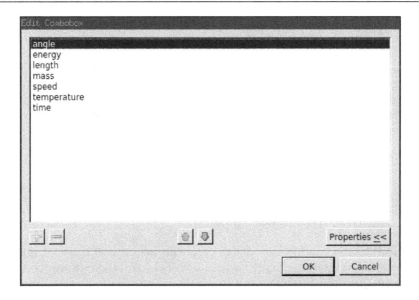

Finally, we will remove the status bar that was automatically added when the user interface was created from the window. This is simply done by right clicking on the bar in **Object Inspector** and clicking **Remove,** as shown in the following screenshot:

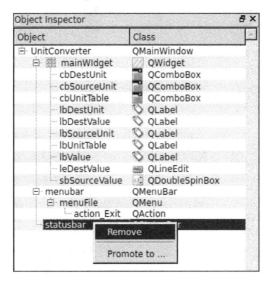

That completes the user interface that we will use for out unit converter application. However, this uses only a small subset of the functionality within the Qt framework for creating the user interfaces.

Writing the UI code

Once the `.ui` file has been created with Qt Designer, we can now write the code that will manage the functionality behind the UI. This will be in a Python file of the same name as the `.ui` file in the `unitconverter.gui` package.

As always, we will start the Python file with the imports for the modules and functions used within the file:

```
import os.path
from PyQt4 import uic
from PyQt4.QtGui import QApplication, QMainWindow
from PyQt4.QtCore import SIGNAL
from ..Converter import get_table
```

Next, we will load the `.ui` file in order to create an instance of the user interface it defines. This is done by replacing the extension of the full file path of the Python source file with `.ui`.

```
ui_filename = os.path.splitext(__file__)[0] + '.ui'
ui_UnitConverter = uic.loadUiType(ui_filename)[0]
```

We will now define a class named `UnitConverter`, which provides the functionality for the user interface. This class will inherit from both `QMainWindow` and the user interface class created when the `.ui` file is loaded.

```
class UnitConverter(QMainWindow, ui_UnitConverter):
    def __init__(self, parent=None):
        QMainWindow.__init__(self, parent)
```

In the constructor of the class, we must setup the user interface layout using the `setupUi` function. This is responsible for actually creating the interface window based on the layout defined in the `.ui` file.

```
        self.setupUi(self)
```

Here, we will connect the `triggered` signal of the **Exit** menu option to the application exit slot in the Qt framework:

```
        self.action_Exit.triggered.connect(QApplication.exit)
```

Here, we will connect the signal of the unit table combo box that notifies the value being changed to the `unit_table_selected` function. We are selecting the version of the signal that provides the option selected as a string (rather than the version that provides the option as an integer index) using the `[str]` syntax.

```
self.cbUnitTable.currentIndexChanged[str].connect
(self.unit_table_selected)
```

Here, we will connect the signals of the source value, the source, and the destination unit input widgets that indicate the selection or value has changed to the `calculate` function in order to update the unit conversion when any of these options is changed.

```
self.cbSourceUnit.currentIndexChanged[str].connect(self.calculate)
        self.cbDestUnit.currentIndexChanged[str].connect(self.
calculate)
        self.sbSourceValue.valueChanged.connect(self.calculate)
```

We will use the `unit_table_selected` function to setup the initial state of the unit selection combo boxes on the user interface:

```
self.unit_table_selected(self.cbUnitTable.currentText())
```

The `unit_table_selected` function is used to handle the selection of a unit table. This function is called when the table selected in the combo box is changed.

```
def unit_table_selected(self, table_name):
```

We will get a list of all units supported by the selected unit table:

```
table = get_table(str(table_name))
units = table.get_units()
```

Next, we will block the Qt signals from being emitted from the two combo boxes used to select the source and the destination units. This prevents the `calculate` function being called unnecessarily when the values in the combo boxes are being updated.

```
self.cbSourceUnit.blockSignals(True)
self.cbDestUnit.blockSignals(True)
```

Now, we will remove all the units in the two combo boxes:

```
self.cbSourceUnit.clear()
self.cbDestUnit.clear()
```

Next, we will add each of the units supported by the current table to each of the combo boxes:

```
for unit in units:
    self.cbSourceUnit.addItem(unit)
    self.cbDestUnit.addItem(unit)
```

Finally, we will allow the two combo boxes to emit the signals once again in order for the application to continue functioning as expected:

```
self.cbSourceUnit.blockSignals(False)
self.cbDestUnit.blockSignals(False)
```

The `calculate` function is used to perform the unit conversion. This takes the values of the unit table, the source value, the source, and the destination units from the widgets in the user interface and performs the calculation using the `convert` function in the `UnitTable` class. Once done, it then sets the test in the destination text box on the user interface.

```
def calculate(self):
    table = get_table(str(self.cbUnitTable.currentText()))
    source_value = self.sbSourceValue.value()
    source_unit = str(self.cbSourceUnit.currentText())
    dest_unit = str(self.cbDestUnit.currentText())
    result_value = table.convert(source_unit, dest_unit, source_
value)
    self.leDestValue.setText(str(result_value))
```

Launching the UI

To launch the UI, we will add a simple function to the `__init__.py` file in the `gui` module:

```
import sys
from PyQt4.QtGui import QApplication
from UnitConverter import UnitConverter
```

The `run_gui` function is used to create a new Qt application and start a new instance of the unit converter user interface. This is the function that will be called by the launch command that we set in the package in the next section.

```
def run_gui():
    app = QApplication(sys.argv)
    ui_window = UnitConverter(None)
    ui_window.show()
    app.exec_()
```

Packaging the code

The last step is to modify the package to include the static files used to define the user interface and add the additional entry point for launching the user interface.

Firstly, we will modify the `entry_points` option to include the `unitconverter-ui` command, as follows:

```
entry_points = {
    'console_scripts': ['unitconvert=unitconverter.CLI:run_cli'],
    'gui_scripts': ['unitconverter-ui=unitconverter.gui:run_gui']
}
```

Next, we will add the `package_data` option to define the static files that we wish to include in the package:

```
package_data = {
    '': ['*.ui']
}
```

In this case, we are including any file with the `.ui` extension anywhere in the package.

 Note that the `package_data` option is technically only required when the `include_package_data` option has not been set to `True`.

Once the package has been modified, it can be installed using the following command:

```
sudo python setup.py install
```

When this completes, you can launch the UI using the following command. Note that you may need to close and re-open the terminal for the command to be recognized after the installation.

```
unitconverter-ui
```

This will open the UI, as shown in the following screenshot. You should now be able to select a combination of unit table, source, and destination units and perform a conversion. The conversion should be performed whenever the source value, the unit table, or either the source or the destination units are changed.

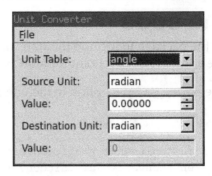

The user interface can now be used to perform unit conversions by selecting a unit table, source, and destination units, and then entering a value in the source value spin box, as shown in the following screenshot:

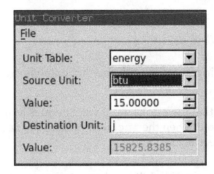

Summary

In this chapter, we looked at how to go about creating a graphical user interface using the Qt framework in Python and extended our unit conversion application to have a graphical interface.

This is the final chapter of this book and by now, I hope you have a good working knowledge of Python and the tools and libraries that come with it. You should now have a try at creating your own scripts and applications using the techniques covered throughout the book.

Index

A

append function 47
Application Protocol Interfaces (APIs) 115
applications, writing for camera
  about 107
  image effect randomizer 112-114
  point and shoot camera 109-112
  timelapse recorder 107, 108
apt
  used, for installing modules 75, 76

B

BeautifulSoup
  used, for parsing webpage 125-130
boolean 32

C

Caesar cipher
  URL 45
camera module
  reference link 101
  setting up 101-105
classes, calculator module
  about 61
  Calculator 62, 63
  Operation 61
classifiers
  about 78
  reference link 78
codebase
  setting up 155, 156

command line interfaces (CLIs)
  about 131
  working on 134-139
control flow operators 36-39

D

data
  downloading, urllib2 used 115, 116
data structures
  about 43
  dictionaries 48
  lists 43, 44
  sets 51
  tuples 54
data types, Python
  about 19-21
  numerical types 21-24
  string manipulation 28
debounceing 93
development tools, Python 13, 14
dictionaries
  about 48
  creating 48, 49
  operations 49, 50
digital electronics 84, 85
Document Object Model (DOM) 120
downloaded operating system image
  writing, to SD card 2
duty cycle 84

E

enum34 package
  URL 74
extend function 47
Extensible Markup Language (XML) 115

Thank you for buying
Getting Started with Python and Raspberry Pi

About Packt Publishing

Packt, pronounced 'packed', published its first book, *Mastering phpMyAdmin for Effective MySQL Management*, in April 2004, and subsequently continued to specialize in publishing highly focused books on specific technologies and solutions.

Our books and publications share the experiences of your fellow IT professionals in adapting and customizing today's systems, applications, and frameworks. Our solution-based books give you the knowledge and power to customize the software and technologies you're using to get the job done. Packt books are more specific and less general than the IT books you have seen in the past. Our unique business model allows us to bring you more focused information, giving you more of what you need to know, and less of what you don't.

Packt is a modern yet unique publishing company that focuses on producing quality, cutting-edge books for communities of developers, administrators, and newbies alike. For more information, please visit our website at www.packtpub.com.

About Packt Open Source

In 2010, Packt launched two new brands, Packt Open Source and Packt Enterprise, in order to continue its focus on specialization. This book is part of the Packt Open Source brand, home to books published on software built around open source licenses, and offering information to anybody from advanced developers to budding web designers. The Open Source brand also runs Packt's Open Source Royalty Scheme, by which Packt gives a royalty to each open source project about whose software a book is sold.

Writing for Packt

We welcome all inquiries from people who are interested in authoring. Book proposals should be sent to author@packtpub.com. If your book idea is still at an early stage and you would like to discuss it first before writing a formal book proposal, then please contact us; one of our commissioning editors will get in touch with you.

We're not just looking for published authors; if you have strong technical skills but no writing experience, our experienced editors can help you develop a writing career, or simply get some additional reward for your expertise.

Raspberry Pi Networking Cookbook

ISBN: 978-1-84969-460-5   Paperback: 204 pages

An epic collection of practical and engaging recipes for the Raspberry Pi!

1. Learn how to install, administer, and maintain your Raspberry Pi.

2. Create a network fileserver for sharing documents, music, and videos.

3. Host a web portal, collaboration wiki, or even your own wireless access point.

4. Connect to your desktop remotely, with minimum hassle.

Learning Raspberry Pi

ISBN: 978-1-78398-282-0   Paperback: 258 pages

Unlock your creative programming potential by creating web technologies, image processing, electronics- and robotics-based projects using the Raspberry Pi

1. Learn how to create games, web, and desktop applications using the best features of the Raspberry Pi.

2. Discover the powerful development tools that allow you to cross-compile your software and build your own Linux distribution for maximum performance.

3. Step-by-step tutorials show you how to quickly develop real-world applications using the Raspberry Pi.

Please check **www.PacktPub.com** for information on our titles

Raspberry Pi Cookbook
for Python Programmers

Over 50 easy-to-comprehend tailor-made recipes to get the
most out of the Raspberry Pi and unleash its huge potential
using Python

Tim Cox

Raspberry Pi Cookbook for Python Programmers

ISBN: 978-1-84969-662-3   Paperback: 402 pages

Over 50 easy-to-comprehend tailor-made recipes to get
the most out of the Raspberry Pi and unleash its huge
potential using Python

1. Install your first operating system, share files
   over the network, and run programs remotely.

2. Unleash the hidden potential of the Raspberry
   Pi's powerful Video Core IV graphics processor
   with your own hardware accelerated 3D
   graphics.

3. Discover how to create your own electronic
   circuits to interact with the Raspberry Pi.

Raspberry Pi Robotic
Projects

Create amazing robotic projects on a shoestring budget

Richard Grimmett

Raspberry Pi Robotic Projects

ISBN: 978-1-84969-432-2   Paperback: 278 pages

Create amazing robotic projects on a shoestring
budget

1. Make your projects talk and understand speech
   with Raspberry Pi.

2. Use standard webcam to make your projects
   see and enhance vision capabilities.

3. Full of simple, easy-to-understand instructions
   to bring your Raspberry Pi online for
   developing robotics projects.

Please check **www.PacktPub.com** for information on our titles